The Parchment Paper COOKBOOK

The Parchment Paper COOKBOOK

180 Healthy, Fast, Delicious Dishes!

NO POTS!
NO PANS!
NO MESS!

Brette Sember

with Nicole Cormier, RD, LDN

Adamsmedia

AVON, MASSACHUSETTS

Published by
Adams Media, a division of F+W Media, Inc.
57 Littlefield Street, Avon, MA 02322. U.S.A.
www.adamsmedia.com

ISBN 10: 1-4405-2859-4
ISBN 13: 978-1-4405-2859-0
eISBN 10: 1-4405-2946-9
eISBN 13: 978-1-4405-2946-7

Printed in the United States of America.

10   9   8   7   6   5   4   3   2   1

Library of Congress Cataloging-in-Publication Data
is available from the publisher.

This publication is designed to provide accurate and authoritative information with regard to the subject matter covered. It is sold with the understanding that the publisher is not engaged in rendering legal, accounting, or other professional advice. If legal advice or other expert assistance is required, the services of a competent professional person should be sought.
—From a *Declaration of Principles* jointly adopted by a Committee of the American Bar Association and a Committee of Publishers and Associations

Many of the designations used by manufacturers and sellers to distinguish their product are claimed as trademarks. Where those designations appear in this book and Adams Media was aware of a trademark claim, the designations have been printed with initial capital letters.

Illustrations by Eric Andrews.

This book is available at quantity discounts for bulk purchases.
For information, please call 1-800-289-0963.

For the women who taught me to cook: Mom, Gai, and Gram.

ACKNOWLEDGMENTS

Thank you to Gina Panettieri for being my agent, advocate, and not least of all, friend, and believing in me and this project. To the wonderful team at Adams Media, including Paula Munier and Casey Ebert, thank you for loving this project as much as I did.

I would likely have not survived the process of writing this without my wonderful circle of writing friends, who are always, always there for me: Sheryl Kraft, Roxanne Hawn, Claudine Jalajas, Peggy Bourjaily, Kris Bordessa, Donna Hull, Ruth Pennebaker, Alisa Bowman, Christine Gross-Loh, Casey Barber, Kristin Gough, Meredith Resnick, Sarah Henry, Alexandra Grabbe, Debbie Koenig, Jane Boursaw, Jennifer Margulis, Jeanine Barone, Judy Stock, Melanie McMinn, Stephanie Auteri, Stephanie Stiavetti, Susan Johnston, Vera Marie Badertscher, and Kerry Dexter.

And to my wonderful husband Terry and our beautiful children Quinne and Zayne, thank you for eating my endless buffet of parchment paper packets and supporting me.

Contents

CHAPTER 3
Pork and Lamb Dishes | 49

CHAPTER 4
Beef and Veal Dishes | 67

CHAPTER 5
Seafood Dishes | 85

CHAPTER 6
Vegetable Dishes | 111

CHAPTER 7
Bread, Rice, and Potato Dishes | 149

CHAPTER 8
Desserts | 173

INTRODUCTION

Cooking with Parchment Paper

I want to let you in on a little secret: parchment paper cooking is the easiest kind of cooking you'll ever do! Think about it . . . no pots, no pans, no dirty baking dishes. No elaborate sauces to stir. No dishpan hands. All of your ingredients go into nifty parchment paper packets, which cook quickly in your oven—or even your toaster oven if you want to save energy. Nothing sticks, nothing crusts, and you have *no cleanup*. Best of all, the end result of this simple cooking method is healthy, flavorful food. Whether you have a small kitchen, an interest in expanding your culinary repertoire, a busy life, or an aversion to washing dishes, the parchment paper method promises to transform how you think about cooking.

No-Pot Benefits

Inside, you won't find one recipe that requires a pot or pan. For many dishes, the parchment paper cooking method allows a delicious sauce to form right inside the packet, so you get all of the flavor with none of the mess associated with traditional cooking. Wrapping your food in parchment paper seals in the moisture and creates a mini–pressure cooker effect, producing incredibly tender meats and fishes; in fact, meals rarely dry out when cooked this way.

Another major benefit: Parchment paper cooking limits the amount of fat you need to add to each dish, making it a healthy way to cook. If going green is important to you, no-pot cooking is environmentally friendly. Not only do you cut down on the amount of water you use to do dishes and the amount of energy needed (since everything cooks in one oven or toaster oven), but you can recycle or compost the parchment paper when you're through with it instead of sending it to the landfill.

Above all, cooking this way allows you to streamline your time in the kitchen, and focus on what really matters—wonderful food, shared with wonderful people.

Parchment Paper 101

Obviously, this method of cooking relies on parchment paper, which you can find in the grocery store, near the rolls of wax paper or foil. (You can also buy it online in bulk; try Amazon or Patterson Paper.) Most grocery stores sell it in rolls, but you can also buy precut sheets in some stores—either will work. Reynolds and Wilton both make parchment paper, as do many other companies, so it should be easy to find. (I don't recommend the precut parchment sheets because they aren't big enough for most recipes in this book—although they are great for the flat parchment recipes.)

The use of parchment dates back to 2500 B.C., when it was made from calfskin and used exclusively for written documents and books. Today's cooking parchment is made of heavy-duty, heat-resistant, nonstick paper. The silicone added to the paper to keep food from sticking also makes it safe to use in the oven, since it will not burn.

The French refer to parchment paper cooking as *en papillote*, which simply means "in paper." Recipes for cooking with paper-product parchment began to emerge around 1910, but most modern cooks have primarily used it as a liner for baking sheets to keep food from sticking—until now.

Preparing for Parchment Paper Cooking

No-pot food prep basically entails layering food in parchment paper packets. (Note that some recipes in the book are meant to be cooked on a flat piece of parchment paper—it doesn't get much easier than that!) Full disclosure: While you won't need baking dishes, pots, or pans, some recipes *do* require the use of a few dishes and utensils. And most recipes use measuring cups and spoons, a knife, cutting board, or a small bowl. Thankfully, these items easily fit into the dishwasher or merely need a wash in the sink, so cleanup's still quick! Some recipes also use the microwave or rice cooker, but since neither of these requires dirtying pots and pans, you're still ahead of the game.

Go for Healthy Options

Throughout this book, you'll notice that many recipes include prepared ingredients readily available at your local market. For this to remain a healthy method of cooking, you need to be careful when selecting these items. Of course, you can always create these ingredients in your own kitchen (using the full range of implements available to you), but if you end up purchasing prepared items, try to opt for the most wholesome choices whenever time and budget permits—choose whole grains over white and buy organic as much as possible. (Steer clear of overly processed foods to boost the health quotient!) I make every effort to use organic food products whenever I can—organic fruits and vegetables have a freshness and sweetness to them that you just don't find in their nonorganic counterparts. And I urge you to try organic, free-range and grass-fed meats; I think you'll be pleasantly surprised. They cook differently and taste better than conventionally raised meat. Organic beef has a

hint of grassiness about it, and organic chicken retains more moisture and has a more satisfying flavor.

Food Notes

All of the chicken recipes in this book call for boneless skinless chicken breasts. Another common ingredient is rice. Brown rice is preferred as it provides more nutritional value and fiber than white rice, but you can always substitute white rice in a pinch. You may want to cook a lot of rice at once and keep it in the fridge to use throughout the week—or freeze it for future use. This easy weekend task will invariably make your weeknight dinners come together that much quicker.

Most recipes call for salt and pepper "to taste." Properly seasoning your food helps make it flavorful, but maybe you follow a low-sodium diet or prefer not to use pepper, so I've left the amounts up to you. When it comes to herbs, most recipes provide measures for dried herbs (when I feel it makes a big difference, I specify fresh herbs), but you can always substitute fresh by using this calculation: 1 tablespoon of fresh herbs equals 1 teaspoon of dried herbs.

These recipes are somewhat loose in an effort to encourage you to modify them to meet your own sensibilities and tastes. For example, if you dislike cilantro, substitute something else (such as parsley); if you dislike goat cheese, swap it out for cream cheese. Experiment with the recipes and make them your own.

One last note, on serving size: Most meat dishes in this book offer amounts for a single serving, which is made in one packet. Make one packet for each person you are feeding. Most side dishes feed four people. You can easily tinker with the serving sizes in the recipes; if a recipe makes one serving, just make additional packets if you want to feed more. If a recipe serves four, cut it in half if you're only cooking for two (but decrease your cooking time accordingly).

Parchment paper packets can also be wrapped in foil and cooked on the grill. If you set your gas grill to medium high heat, the cooking times should be very similar to the times for cooking in the oven, but be sure to check your food for doneness. It also is useful to turn your packets on the grill once to ensure even cooking.

Folding the Parchment

Despite what you may think, you don't need to be an origami artist to cook this way— there are no elaborate swans involved! Simply follow these folding methods and you're on your way.

(For most single-serving dishes in this book, use a 20" piece of parchment; when making family-size recipes, use a 30" piece.)

1. First, be sure to arrange your food so that you have at least 4" of paper on the sides (along the long edges) and at least 5" along the ends (the short edges).
2. You want the food centered on the paper and flattened so it is of even thickness throughout.
3. Lift up the ends of the paper (the short edges) and bring them together in the center of the food.
4. Fold them over at least twice (creasing the folds so they hold) so that you fold directly down tight to the food, making sure your fold goes all the way out to the short ends.
5. To fold the sides, you can either simply twist each end (nothing delicate required here, just twist it up) or you can fold it like you would

a wrapped gift, bringing the long sides in to meet at a 'v' and then just folding in toward the food a few times.

6. It's important to tightly fold the paper so that there isn't a lot of extra space around the food and none of the juices leak out.

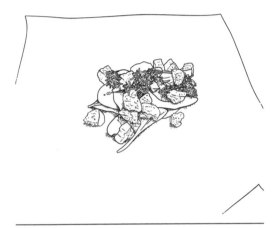

1. Place the food in the center of the parchment.

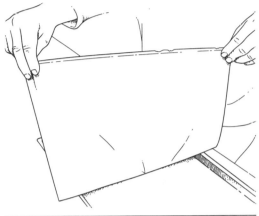

2. Take each of the short ends of the paper and hold them up so they meet in the middle, above the food.

3. Fold these edges together, creasing them.

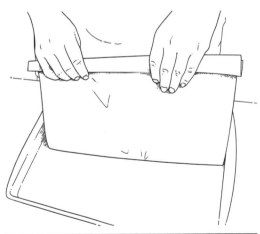

4. Continue folding these edges over and over, creasing it each time.

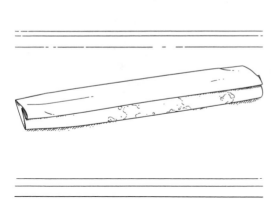

5. Fold down until you reach the food.

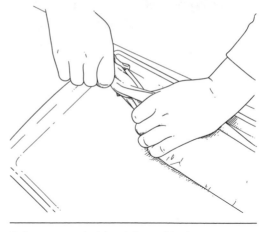

6. Grasp one end of the packet and begin twisting it.

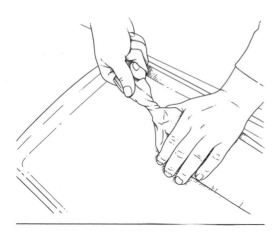

7. Continue twisting.

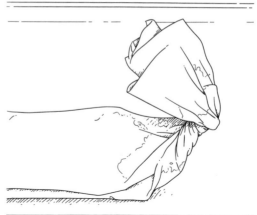

8. Finish twisting so the end of the twist is facing up. Repeat for the other side.

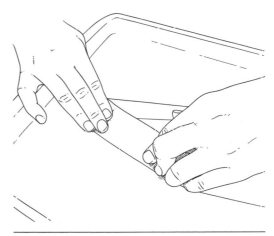

9. For an alternate method, take one end of the paper and fold one side of it in, like a triangle. Crease the paper.

10. Fold the other side in and crease the paper.

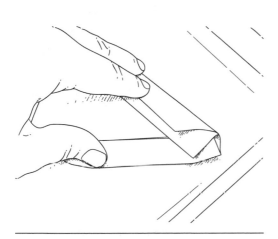

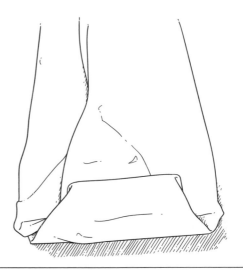

11. The edges should make a triangle.

12. Now fold the point up, folding several times and creasing, until the end of the packet is secure.

Techniques for Success

In general, it's a good idea to place your parchment paper packets on a baking sheet lined with foil. While it's extremely unlikely that the parchment paper will leak, I recommend using the foil because the paper can get damp on the bottom and could slightly dirty your baking sheet. Also, the foil gives you added insurance should the parchment paper ever rip (it never has for me). Don't worry, you can reuse the same piece of foil over and over (since it's not likely to get dirty), and foil is also recyclable. If you don't have a baking sheet, you can place some of the sturdier packets (wrapped very securely in foil so they cannot possibly leak) directly on an oven or toaster oven rack—but be sure you can transport it without it tearing or breaking open and be careful it doesn't leak.

While all of the cooking times have been tested, this isn't an exact science—common sense comes into play. If you use a chicken breast or piece of fish that is quite thick, you will likely need to cook it a bit longer than the recipe says. And if you use one that is quite thin, it'll probably take less time to cook. Layering your food in the packet in a consistent and even way will help the food cook evenly. If you want to check your food

for doneness (particularly useful with meat), pull it out of the oven, wait about ten seconds so the paper cools enough to touch, and gently unfold the paper over the center of the food to peek in. Be careful not to burn yourself on the hot steam that will come out of the packet. If you need to cook the food longer, just refold along the creases. You can also leave the packet closed and poke an instant-read thermometer through the paper.

> The U.S. Department of Agriculture recommends that you cook chicken to 165°F, beef to 145°F, ground beef to 160°F, eggs to 160°F, fish to 145°F, ground lamb to 160°F, lamb chops to 140°F, and pork to 145°F.

Some recipes instruct you to open up your packet and then quickly broil the food. **While parchment paper is safe for oven baking, you need to be careful if you broil.** First, open the packet and flatten the parchment paper so it lays flat on the pan and does not stick up (tucking the edges underneath the packet makes this easy). Or cut off the parchment that is not under the food. Always put your tray in the middle of the oven—NOT the shelf closest to the heat source. Second, always stay by your oven with a close eye on the parchment. You will never need to broil for more than a minute or two, which is usually sufficient to brown your food. Parchment paper will brown (which is actually a very pretty effect) and char if it gets hot, but will not burn.

Serving Your Parchment Paper Creation

When it comes to serving, of course you can open the packets, take out the food, and place it in serving dishes. However, for weeknight family meals when you want to minimize cleanup, you can place individual packets on each person's plate (food also stays warmer if it's kept in the packets).

But don't think that no-pot cooking is only for family night! Impress your guests by serving individual parchment paper packets at your next dinner party. It's like a personalized restaurant experience unfolding before their eyes—because opening up a parchment packet of steaming, aromatic, and flavorful food feels like opening the most delicious present.

CHAPTER 1

Breakfast Dishes

Mornings are often a busy time, but breakfast is important. The recipes in this chapter offer some quick ideas for a hot breakfast without a lot of effort or cleanup. With many of the breakfast sandwiches, you can just leave them in the parchment and take them with you as you dash out the door.

Breakfast Sandwich

Serves 1

Here's a much better option than a breakfast sandwich from a fast-food place. Eggs, sausage, cheese, and seasoning make this a delicious start to the day—one that's also portable and just as good when cold.

1 6" sub sandwich roll, preferably whole wheat

1 egg

¼ teaspoon Italian seasoning

Salt and pepper to taste

1 low-fat precooked breakfast sausage link

¼ cup extra-sharp Cheddar cheese

Ketchup or hot sauce

1. Preheat oven to 400°F.
2. Cut a 20" piece of parchment.
3. Line a baking sheet with aluminum foil.
4. Cut the roll in half, lengthwise.
5. Take the bottom of the roll and scoop out as much of the soft inside bread as you can, leaving the outline of the roll intact.
6. Place the bottom of the roll on the parchment.
7. In a small bowl, mix one egg with Italian seasoning, salt, and pepper.
8. Pour into bottom of roll.
9. Crumble the sausage over the egg.
10. Top with cheese.
11. Place the top of the roll onto the sandwich.
12. Fold the parchment.
13. Bake for 22 minutes.
14. Remove from oven, open the sandwich, and top with ketchup, hot sauce, or both.

Stick this in the oven while you get dressed for the day and voila! Instant breakfast. Take it along with you in its parchment wrapper on your commute, or enjoy at home while you watch the morning shows.

Calories: 396 | Fat: 24 g | Protein: 24 g | Sodium: 617 mg | Carbohydrates: 21 g | Fiber: 1.6 g

Eggs in a Nest

Serves 4

This colorful dish is lovely for brunch or dinner. Children love discovering the eggs tucked into the nests, while the Swiss chard makes this a very grown-up meal.

1 bunch Swiss chard, stems removed, and roughly chopped

3 cloves garlic, chopped

2 cups cooked, refrigerated hash browns (sold in the dairy section)

4 eggs

Salt and pepper to taste

2 slices Swiss cheese, torn or roughly chopped

1. Preheat oven to 400ºF.

2. Cut a 20" piece of parchment.

3. Line a baking sheet with aluminum foil.

4. Place the Swiss chard on the parchment in about an 8" circle.

5. Sprinkle garlic on top.

6. Add hash browns and toss to combine.

7. Make 4 small "nests" in the chard and put an egg (removed from its shell) in each spot. Sprinkle with salt and pepper.

8. Top with Swiss cheese.

9. Fold the parchment.

10. Bake for 20 minutes, until the whites of the eggs are set but the yolks are still runny.

Calories: 226 | Fat: 10 g | Protein: 13 g | Sodium: 215 mg | Carbohydrates: 23 g | Fiber: 2 g

Banana Pecan Pancake Sandwich

Serves 1

This sandwich is portable and tastes great whether it's fresh out of the oven or has cooled a bit. Add peanut butter to this and it becomes an Elvis breakfast sandwich, which also gives it a protein boost. Be sure to use real maple syrup rather than "pancake syrup."

2 frozen pancakes (preferably whole grain), defrosted

2 teaspoons maple syrup

½ banana, cut into lengthwise strips

4 pecans, chopped

1. Preheat oven to 400°F.
2. Cut a 20" piece of parchment.
3. Line a baking sheet with aluminum foil.
4. Spread 1 teaspoon syrup on one side of each pancake.
5. Place one pancake on parchment, syrup side up, and top with banana, then pecans, pressing the pecans down into the banana.
6. Top with the other pancake.
7. Fold the parchment.
8. Bake for 13 minutes.

Calories: 333 | Fat: 9 g | Protein: 6 g | Sodium: 412 mg | Carbohydrates: 58 g | Fiber: 5 g

Lazy Man's Quiche

Serves 3 or 4

This recipe was inspired by the free-form Rustic Apple Tart dessert in this book (see Chapter 8). After all, if a pie can be free-form, why not a quiche? I love the fact that there is no pie pan to wash!

1 refrigerated unbaked pie crust

5 eggs

4 tablespoons skim milk

½ cup fat-free feta cheese

½ cup diced tomatoes

¼ cup frozen spinach, defrosted and squeezed dry

¼ teaspoon Greek seasoning (or oregano)

¼ teaspoon onion powder

Salt and pepper to taste

1. Preheat oven to 400°F.

2. Cut a 20" piece of parchment and place on a baking sheet.

3. Lay the pie crust down on the parchment and scrunch up the edges of the crust so you have a square that is about 6" or 7" on each side.

4. Scrunch the sides up so they create a barrier to hold the egg in.

5. You can mix the eggs and milk in a small bowl or crack the eggs right onto the pie crust and then add the milk to them, mixing gently with a fork. You just want to break the yolks and combine the egg with the milk only enough so that it is slightly mixed.

6. Sprinkle the rest of the ingredients over the egg mixture.

7. Fold up the edges of the parchment.

8. Bake for 18–20 minutes or until the egg is set.

Try different ingredients for variety. Ham, mushrooms, tomato, other cheese, salsa, or other herbs all add a new dimension to this savory egg dish.

Calories: 304 | Fat: 17 g | Protein: 13.5 g | Sodium: 434 mg | Carbohydrates: 19.5 g | Fiber: 1 g

Breakfast Croissant Sandwich

Serves 1

This warm and flaky sandwich satisfies on a busy morning but also works for lunch or a light dinner paired with a green salad and some melon. The prosciutto adds a wonderful salty flavor.

3 slices prosciutto

1 croissant

Honey mustard to taste

2 slices ripe tomato (¼" thick)

1 slice fontina cheese

1. Preheat oven to 400ºF.
2. Cut a 20" piece of parchment.
3. Place parchment on a baking sheet and lay the prosciutto flat on it (don't fold the parchment). Bake for 9 minutes.
4. Cut the croissant in half and spread with mustard.
5. Layer the prosciutto, tomato, and cheese on the sandwich.
6. Fold the parchment.
7. Bake for 10 minutes.

Calories: 388 | Fat: 29 g | Protein: 17 g | Sodium: 863 mg | Carbohydrates: 15 g | Fiber: 1 g

Eggs Almost Benedict

Serves 1

This portable sandwich mimics traditional eggs Benedict, which features a hollandaise sauce. In this recipe, the cream cheese provides the creaminess of that sauce with the addition of onion flavor.

1 whole wheat bagel

1 egg

Salt and pepper to taste

1 tablespoon frozen chopped spinach, defrosted and squeezed dry

1 slice Canadian bacon

1 tablespoon light chive and onion cream cheese

1. Preheat oven to 400°F.
2. Cut a 20" piece of parchment.
3. Line a baking sheet with aluminum foil.
4. Cut off the top third of the bagel; set aside to use as a "lid."
5. Take the bottom half and scoop out most of the soft inside, making sure to leave the outside edges and the edges around the inside hole intact.
6. Crack the egg in a small bowl, then pour into the bagel, tipping the bagel to spread it around but leaving the yolk intact.
7. Season with salt and pepper.
8. Sprinkle spinach on top.
9. Place the Canadian bacon on top.
10. Spread the cream cheese on the inside of the "lid."
11. Place the lid on top of the egg-filled bagel.
12. Fold the parchment.
13. Bake for 25 minutes.

Canadian bacon (also called back bacon) is not really bacon at all but a cut of ham that comes from the side loin. Leaner than bacon, it makes a great healthy substitute.

Calories: 271 | Fat: 8 g | Protein: 19 g | Sodium: 710 mg | Carbohydrates: 31 g | Fiber: 3 g

Italian Sausage Strata

Serves 4

A lovely brunch dish, the savory flavors also make this ideal for dinner, paired with a bright green salad or a bowl of vegetable soup. I use Italian turkey sausage in this, but you can substitute any kind of sausage you like.

4 thick slices of crusty bread

3 eggs

¾ cup skim milk

Salt and pepper to taste

1 cup shredded part-skim mozzarella cheese

2 Italian turkey sausages, removed from their casing

¼ teaspoon dry mustard

1 tablespoon Italian seasoning

6 Baby Bella or white mushrooms, sliced

2 tablespoons chopped onion

1 tablespoon Parmesan cheese

1. Preheat oven to 400°F.
2. Cut a 20" piece of parchment and spray center with cooking spray.
3. Line a baking sheet with aluminum foil.
4. Cut the bread into cubes.
5. In a medium bowl, mix eggs and milk.
6. Add the bread cubes to the bowl and mix.
7. Add salt and pepper.
8. Add cheese, sausage, dry mustard, Italian seasoning, mushrooms, and onion.
9. Stir to mix and allow it to rest about 5 minutes.
10. Place mixture in the center of the parchment in about a 6" × 6" square of even thickness.
11. Fold the parchment.
12. Bake 40 minutes.
13. Open the parchment and sprinkle the top with the Parmesan cheese. Broil for 2 minutes.

A mix of bread, egg, milk, cheese, and other ingredients, strata is moist and flavorful when baked. Traditionally soaked for several hours, this version saves you a lot of time.

Calories: 357 | Fat: 16 g | Protein: 26 g | Sodium: 734 mg | Carbohydrates: 26 g | Fiber: 2 g

Baked Oatmeal

Serves 1

While nourishing and filling, oatmeal can become a bit boring for breakfast. Jazz up your morning meal with this fun baked oatmeal—a favorite with kids.

1 package instant maple and brown sugar oatmeal, mixed with hot water as directed

1 individual serving applesauce container (4 ounces)

¼ cup granola

1. Preheat oven to 400ºF.

2. Cut a 20" piece of parchment.

3. Place the parchment on a baking sheet and spray the middle of the parchment paper with cooking spray.

4. Pour the oatmeal in the center of the parchment.

5. Pour applesauce on top.

6. Sprinkle with granola.

7. Fold the parchment.

8. Bake for 15 minutes.

You can substitute plain instant oats for the packaged oatmeal. Follow the package directions to make one serving, then add any flavors—cinnamon, sugar, maple syrup, honey—that you like.

Calories: 323 | Fat: 9 g | Protein: 7 g | Sodium: 256 mg | Carbohydrates: 53 g | Fiber: 5.5 g

Bibimbap

Serves 1

A Korean rice dish, Bibimbap makes a wonderfully healthy and satisfying breakfast. This dish is colorful and beautiful to look at with its different colored "zones!"

1 cup cooked brown rice

½ small zucchini, sliced thin

1 carrot or 4 baby carrots, sliced thin

3 tablespoons chopped onion

2 white or Baby Bella mushrooms, sliced thin

1 egg

Salt and pepper to taste

2 teaspoons sesame oil

Korean hot chili paste

Tamari or soy sauce

1. Preheat oven to 400ºF.

2. Cut a 20" piece of parchment.

3. Line a baking sheet with aluminum foil.

4. Place rice in a 4"–5" circle on the parchment, creating a well in the middle.

5. Place the zucchini, carrots, onion, and mushroom each in its own quadrant on top of the rice, leaving the middle well empty.

6. Break the egg into the well in the center.

7. Season with salt and pepper.

8. Drizzle sesame oil over everything.

9. Fold the parchment.

10. Bake for 12–15 minutes, until the egg white is set but the yolk is still runny.

11. Serve with Korean hot chili paste and/or tamari (or soy sauce).

Calories: 856 | Fat: 16 g | Protein: 12 g | Sodium: 105 mg | Carbohydrates: 50 g | Fiber: 5 g

Polenta Egg Bake

Serves 1

Use store-bought, refrigerated polenta that comes in a tube for this recipe. You can also make your own, roll into a tube shape, and refrigerate in plastic wrap. If you can't find Italian flavored, just use plain and add ½ teaspoon of Italian herbs to the dish. The interesting mix of ingredients is an eye-opening way to start your day.

4 slices (each ½" thick) premade Italian-flavored polenta from a tube

1 egg

1 slice ripe tomato (½" thick), quartered

Salt and pepper to taste

1. Preheat the oven to 400°F.

2. Cut a 20" piece of parchment.

3. Line a baking sheet with aluminum foil.

4. Place the polenta slices in a square on the parchment.

5. Break the egg on top of the polenta.

6. Place a quarter slice of tomato at the edge of each polenta slice.

7. Season with salt and pepper to taste.

8. Fold the parchment.

9. Bake 11–13 minutes, until the egg is set.

Calories: 181 | Fat: 3 g | Protein: 8.5 g | Sodium: 63 mg | Carbohydrates: 24 g | Fiber: 0 g

Spicy Breakfast Sandwich

Serves 1

Featured in many spicy Indian and British dishes, hot mango chutney wakes your mouth in this surprising breakfast sandwich! Feel free to substitute any type of cheese you like or use ham in place of the Canadian bacon.

1 whole wheat English muffin

1 slice Canadian bacon

1 slice ripe tomato (½" thick)

1 slice Colby jack cheese

1 teaspoon hot mango chutney

1. Preheat oven to 400°F.
2. Cut a 20" piece of parchment.
3. Line a baking sheet with aluminum foil.
4. Spray the outsides of the English muffin with cooking spray and place one half on the parchment.
5. Top with Canadian bacon, tomato, and cheese.
6. Spread chutney on remaining half of the English muffin and place on top of sandwich.
7. Fold the parchment.
8. Bake for 15 minutes.

If you have an international section in your grocery store, look in the Indian or British section. In a pinch, peach preserves with a dash of hot sauce tastes remarkably similar. Mango chutney can be found in the preserves section of your grocery store.

Calories: 317 | Fat: 12 g | Protein: 18 g | Sodium: 676 mg | Carbohydrates: 35 g | Fiber: 2 g

Brunch Strata

Serves 4

Perfect for brunch served alongside a fresh fruit salad, this strata comes together in a snap. Try using mushrooms in place of spinach for an earthier flavor, and feel free to substitute another kind of ham for Canadian bacon if you like.

3 eggs

¾ cup skim milk

4 thick slices crusty whole wheat bread, cubed

Salt and pepper to taste

2 scallions, chopped green and white parts

¼ cup frozen chopped spinach, defrosted and squeezed dry

3 slices Canadian bacon, cubed

¼ red bell pepper, diced

½ cup shredded sharp Cheddar cheese

½ cup shredded smoked Gouda cheese

¼ teaspoon dried thyme

¼ teaspoon dry mustard

1 tablespoon Parmesan cheese

1. Preheat oven to 400°F.
2. Cut a 20" piece of parchment and spray center with cooking spray.
3. Line a baking sheet with aluminum foil.
4. Mix eggs and milk in a medium bowl and add bread.
5. Stir to mix.
6. Add salt and pepper to taste.
7. Add scallions, spinach, Canadian bacon, red pepper, cheeses, thyme, and dry mustard to the egg mixture.
8. Combine thoroughly.
9. Allow to rest about 5 minutes.
10. Place on parchment in about a 6" × 6" square.
11. Fold the parchment.
12. Bake for 40 minutes.
13. Open parchment, sprinkle Parmesan on top, and broil for 2 minutes.

Calories: 390 | Fat: 20 g | Protein: 25 g | Sodium: 793 mg | Carbohydrates: 25 g | Fiber: 3 g

Deviled Egg Waffle Sandwich

Serves 1

Waffles and eggs are traditional breakfast items, but put them together and you've got something fun and new. This combines the taste of deviled eggs in an easy-to-eat waffle sandwich.

2 whole-grain waffles (regular size, not Belgian)

1 hard-boiled egg, chopped

1 tablespoon light mayonnaise

½ teaspoon yellow mustard

⅛ teaspoon onion powder

Salt and pepper to taste

Pinch of paprika

1 teaspoon of the green end of a scallion, chopped

1 thin slice deli ham

1. Preheat oven to 400°F.

2. Cut a 20" piece of parchment.

3. Line a baking sheet with aluminum foil.

4. Spray one side of a waffle with cooking spray and place sprayed side down on the parchment.

5. In a small bowl mix egg, mayonnaise, mustard, onion powder, salt, pepper, paprika, and scallion.

6. Spread this mixture onto the waffle.

7. Top with a slice of ham and the second waffle.

8. Spray the top of the waffle with cooking spray.

9. Fold the parchment.

10. Bake for 17 minutes.

Calories: 339 | Fat: 17 g | Protein: 14 g | Sodium: 816 mg | Carbohydrates: 33 g | Fiber: 3 g

CHAPTER 2

Chicken and Turkey Dishes

Tired of the same old poultry dishes? Many people find they just repeat the same few recipes over and over throughout the month. The offerings in this chapter provide lots of new ideas and some twists on standards, all cooked in parchment, leaving you with almost no cleanup. What a lifesaver on a busy weeknight! You can also enjoy these dishes for relaxed weekend dinners when you're in the mood for something fun, or when you know you'll be making other, more complicated dishes along with these. After all, there's no need for the entire meal to be complicated!

Chicken Français

Serves 4

Sometimes the simplest dishes are the most delicious. The capers in this dish add a wonderful savory flavor. Serve this with a salad and a loaf of warm French bread.

3 tablespoons melted butter

3 tablespoons white wine

Juice of 1 lemon

1 teaspoon cornstarch

Salt and pepper to taste

½ teaspoon dried thyme or several sprigs of fresh thyme

4 boneless skinless chicken breasts

2 teaspoons capers

1. Mix butter, wine, lemon juice, cornstarch, salt, and pepper in a small bowl.

2. If using dried thyme, add it to the mixture.

3. Transfer marinade to a zip-top bag and add the chicken.

4. Refrigerate for at least half an hour (or up to one day ahead).

5. You can create this dish as two packets with two servings each, or as four individual packets. (Cut two pieces of 20-inch-long parchment, or four pieces that are 12-inches long.)

6. Line a baking sheet with foil and preheat oven to 400°F.

7. Place chicken on the parchment.

8. Pour marinade over the chicken. Sprinkle with capers.

9. If you are using fresh thyme, lay a sprig on top of each piece of chicken.

10. Fold the parchment.

11. Bake for 20 minutes.

I love to make extras of this chicken dish and eat the leftovers in salads for weekday lunches. It's also great on a sandwich (try it on a croissant) with some lettuce, tomato, mustard, and mayo.

Calories: 256 | Fat: 12 g | Protein: 33 g | Sodium: 208 mg | Carbohydrates: 1 g | Fiber: 0 g

Cream of Chicken Crepe

Serves 1

Rotisserie or leftover chicken makes this a quick meal to put together. Jazz it up with some spinach, mushrooms, or fresh herbs for added flavor. Make as many crepes as you like together in one packet, but increase the cooking time by about 5 minutes if you have more than three crepes.

½ cup cooked shredded chicken (rotisserie or leftover)

1 crepe (store-bought or homemade)

2 tablespoons skim milk

1 teaspoon cornstarch

1 tablespoon Parmesan cheese

2 tablespoons butter

⅛ teaspoon garlic powder

Salt and pepper to taste

1 tablespoon fresh parsley

1. Preheat oven to 400°F.
2. Cut a 20" piece of parchment.
3. Line a baking sheet with aluminum foil.
4. Place chicken on one side of the crepe.
5. In a small glass bowl, combine milk, cornstarch, and cheese. Add butter.
6. Heat in the microwave about 15 seconds and stir until butter is melted and mixture is thickened.
7. Stir in garlic powder, salt, pepper, and parsley.
8. Spoon half of the sauce over the chicken.
9. Roll up the crepe and place seam-side down on the parchment.
10. Spoon the rest of the sauce on top of the crepe.
11. Fold the parchment.
12. Bake for 10 minutes.
13. Open the parchment and broil for 2–3 minutes, until it browns on top.

You can normally find prepared crepes in the refrigerated produce section of the grocery store. They are delicious and easy to work with, but if you're feeling so inclined, you could also make them from scratch.

Calories: 381 | Fat: 27 g | Protein: 16 g | Sodium: 511 mg | Carbohydrates: 19 g | Fiber: 1 g

Chicken Dijon

Serves 4

A staple condiment, Dijon mustard can transform simple dishes with sublime sauces. Packed with flavor, the leftovers from this dish work wonderfully in a salad the next day. If you have fresh tarragon, use that instead (1 teaspoon of dried herbs equals 1 tablespoon of fresh).

4 boneless skinless chicken breasts

3 tablespoons Dijon mustard

1 tablespoon olive oil

2 tablespoons white wine

2 tablespoons light mayonnaise

1 teaspoon dried tarragon

Salt and pepper to taste

Fresh parsley

1. Preheat the oven to 400ºF.

2. Cut four 20" pieces of parchment.

3. Line a baking sheet with aluminum foil.

4. Place the chicken breasts on four pieces of parchment paper.

5. Mix mustard, olive oil, white wine, mayo, and tarragon in a small bowl. Spread the sauce on top of the chicken, dividing it among the packets.

6. Season each with salt and pepper and top with a sprig of parsley.

7. Fold the parchment.

8. Bake for 20 minutes.

Calories: 165 | Fat: 7 g | Protein: 20 g | Sodium: 67 mg | Carbohydrates: 1.5 g | Fiber: 0 g

Turkey Meatloaf

Serves 4

I stopped making meatloaf with ground beef years ago—I prefer turkey because it's lighter and takes on the flavor of the spices. This version uses oats and whole wheat bread to give it body.

½ cup rolled oats (quick cooking or old-fashioned)

2 tablespoons skim milk

1 pound ground turkey, 99% fat free

1 teaspoon olive oil

2 tablespoons sweet Asian chili sauce

1 tablespoon Worcestershire sauce

1 tablespoon ketchup

½ teaspoon dry mustard

1 egg

2 tablespoons sweet and sour sauce plus ⅛ cup (reserve the ⅛ cup)

½ small onion, chopped (about ¼ cup)

1 chopped garlic clove

1 slice whole wheat bread, ripped into small pieces

Salt and pepper to taste

1. Preheat oven to 400°F.
2. Cut a 20" piece of parchment.
3. Line a baking sheet with aluminum foil.
4. Place the oats in the bowl and cover with the milk, allowing it to soak for about 2 minutes.
5. Add all the other ingredients, except the ⅛ cup of sweet and sour sauce, and mix.
6. Place the meatloaf mixture onto a piece of parchment and form into a loaf shape.
7. Brush reserved ⅛ cup sweet and sour sauce on top.
8. Fold the parchment.
9. Bake for 45 minutes.

The sweet and sour sauce and sweet Asian chili sauce in this recipe amps up the flavor. You can find the chili sauce in the Asian section of your grocery store.

Calories: 240 | Fat: 5 g | Protein: 32 g | Sodium: 202 mg | Carbohydrates: 23 g | Fiber: 3 g

Chicken Stuffed with Artichokes and Cheese

Serves 1

There's a reason the artichoke dip never sticks around for long; the vegetable and cheese combo is a match made in heaven. In this recipe, the pairing is stuffed inside the chicken breast and tastes incredibly complicated, but is actually very simple to make.

1 boneless skinless chicken breast

4 or 5 quartered artichoke hearts (from a frozen bag, defrosted)

1 tablespoon chive and onion cream cheese

1 tablespoon grated fontina cheese

Salt and pepper to taste

¼ teaspoon Italian seasoning

½ tablespoon seasoned bread crumbs

⅛ teaspoon garlic powder

1. Preheat oven to 400°F.
2. Cut a 20" piece of parchment.
3. Line a baking sheet with aluminum foil.
4. Lay the chicken breast on the parchment.
5. Place your hand on top of it.
6. With a knife parallel to your hand, make a slit in one of the long sides of the breast, being careful not to cut all the way through to the other side. Make the slit as deep and as long as possible.
7. In a food processor, chop the remaining ingredients.
8. Fill the pocket with the mixture and place any that remains on top of the chicken.
9. Season the outside of the chicken with salt and pepper.
10. Fold the parchment.
11. Bake for 20 minutes.

Calories: 327 | Fat: 9 g | Protein: 43 g | Sodium: 351 mg | Carbohydrates: 20 g | Fiber: 9 g

Barbecue Chicken and Beans

Serves 4

If your kids love baked beans, you'll want to work this dish into your family's reper-toire. I strongly urge you to use organic ketchup for this; it has a very different flavor. This dish pairs wonderfully with coleslaw, followed by a fruity finish such as Clemen-tine Tart (see Chapter 8).

2 boneless skinless chicken breasts, each cut into halves

1 cup canned baked beans (prefera-bly organic, in a tomato-based sauce)

½ cup ketchup

2 tablespoons brown sugar (dark or light will work)

¼ teaspoon garlic powder

1 teaspoon apple cider vinegar

½ teaspoon Worcestershire sauce

1 teaspoon yellow mustard

1. Preheat oven to 400°F.

2. Cut two 20" pieces of parchment for two packets of two servings each, or four 12" pieces.

3. Line a baking sheet with foil.

4. Place chicken on the parchment and cover with baked beans

5. Mix remaining ingredients in a small bowl and pour over the top, dividing evenly among the packets.

6. Fold the parchment.

7. Bake for 40 minutes.

Calories: 224 | Fat: 2.5 g | Protein: 24 g | Sodium: 524 mg | Carbohydrates: 28 g | Fiber: 3 g

Chicken with Sage, Brown Butter, and Sweet Potatoes

Serves 1

The brightly colored potatoes make this a visually pleasing dish. Sage gives it a warm and comforting flavor, and the brown butter adds a nutty taste that keeps you coming back for more. Use white-flesh sweet potatoes if you prefer them to the yellow-orange fleshed varieties.

1 boneless skinless chicken breast

½ sweet potato, washed and thinly sliced

2 tablespoons brown butter

⅛ teaspoon dried sage

Salt and pepper to taste

Sprig fresh parsley (optional)

1. Preheat oven to 400°F.
2. Cut a 20" piece of parchment.
3. Line a baking sheet with aluminum foil.
4. Place the chicken in the center of the parchment.
5. Arrange the potato slices on top.
6. Pour the butter over the chicken and potato.
7. Sprinkle sage, salt, and pepper on top.
8. Place sprig of parsley on top.
9. Fold the parchment.
10. Bake for 22 minutes. Allow the packet to rest about 3 minutes before opening.

Brown butter is just that, butter that has been cooked until it browns. Melt the butter in a small glass dish in the microwave for about 1½ minutes, stirring frequently, until it turns a nutty brown but does not burn. It has amazing flavor. I especially enjoy it on steamed veggies.

Calories: 366 | Fat: 25 g | Protein: 22 g | Sodium: 318 mg | Carbohydrates: 13 g | Fiber: 2 g

Chicken Tagine

Serves 1

The exotic flavors of this dish gives it the feeling of something really special and different. As you peel open the colorful packet, you'll feel transported to a faraway land.

½ cup cooked brown rice

1 boneless skinless chicken breast

2 tablespoons diced canned or fresh tomato

1 tablespoon juice from tomato can

1 tablespoon canned garbanzo beans

Salt and pepper to taste

¼ teaspoon dried chopped/minced onion

⅛ teaspoon cumin

⅛ teaspoon cinnamon

Pinch of red pepper flakes

1 tablespoon white wine

1 teaspoon olive oil

4 dried apricot halves, roughly chopped

Sprig of fresh parsley (optional)

1. Preheat oven to 400°F.
2. Cut a 20" piece of parchment.
3. Line a baking sheet with aluminum foil.
4. Place the rice on the parchment and lay the chicken breast on top.
5. Pile remaining ingredients on top in the order listed.
6. Fold the parchment.
7. Bake for 22 minutes. Allow the packet to rest three minutes before opening it.

Tagine is a traditional North African dish, named after the distinctive vessel in which it's cooked. The clay dish has a dome-shaped lid with an opening at the top. Here you can enjoy the flavors of a tagine without the clay dish—or the cleanup.

Calories: 293 | Fat: 7.5 g | Protein: 23 g | Sodium: 182 mg | Carbohydrates: 20 g | Fiber: 2.6 g

Chicken with Squash and Apple

Serves 1

The homey flavor of the squash and apple pairing in this dish will warm you up on a cold fall night. Serve alongside a spinach salad for a complete meal. You can substitute butternut squash for the acorn squash if you prefer.

½ cup cooked brown rice

1 boneless skinless chicken breast

½ cup peeled, roughly chopped acorn squash

½ of an apple, cored and roughly chopped

1 teaspoon olive oil

⅛ teaspoon cinnamon

1 teaspoon thyme

Pinch dried mustard

Salt and pepper to taste

1 tablespoon apple juice or cider

1 teaspoon apple cider vinegar

1. Preheat oven to 400°F.
2. Cut a 20" piece of parchment.
3. Line a baking sheet with aluminum foil.
4. Place the rice on the parchment and lay the chicken breast on top.
5. Place the squash and apple on top.
6. Drizzle with the olive oil; sprinkle on the cinnamon, thyme, and dried mustard.
7. Season with salt and pepper.
8. Drizzle on the juice or cider and vinegar.
9. Fold the parchment.
10. Bake 22 minutes. Allow the packet to rest about 3 minutes before opening.

Acorn squash is one of my favorite types of squash. It's round, green, and ridged. It's easier to peel and cut up than butternut squash (cut it into wedges and then just cut the skin off) and has a lovely orange/yellow color inside.

Calories: 290 | Fat: 7 g | Protein: 22 g | Sodium: 53 mg | Carbohydrates: 20 g | Fiber: 3 g

Greek Chicken

Serves 1

My family loves to go out for souvlaki, but this chicken dish is my replacement when I want to stay home or restaurant meals are not in the budget. Serve this with some warm whole wheat pitas or some potatoes cooked with Greek seasoning.

1 boneless skinless chicken breast

1 teaspoon olive oil

Salt and pepper to taste (use more than you think you need)

⅛ teaspoon onion powder

1 whole canned tomato (from a can of whole tomatoes)

¼ cup fat-free feta cheese

4 quartered artichoke hearts from a can (or freezer bag, defrosted)

⅛ teaspoon Greek seasoning

½ teaspoon lemon juice

Sprig of fresh parsley and oregano (optional)

Sliced black olives (optional)

1. Preheat oven to 400°F.
2. Cut a 20" piece of parchment.
3. Line a baking sheet with aluminum foil.
4. Place the chicken breast on the parchment.
5. Drizzle olive oil on top and season with salt, pepper, and onion powder.
6. Top with tomato, feta cheese, and artichoke.
7. Sprinkle Greek seasoning on top, then drizzle with lemon juice.
8. Top with fresh herbs if you have them.
9. Top with olives if using.
10. Fold the parchment.
11. Bake for 20 minutes. Let the package rest 3–4 minutes before serving.

> Greek seasoning is a combination of herbs such as oregano, lemon zest, and garlic. You can buy it from Penzeys Spices (www.penzeys.com) or make your own to your own tastes.

Calories: 341 | Fat: 16 g | Protein: 32 g | Sodium: 728 mg | Carbohydrates: 23 g | Fiber: 5 g

Chicken with Mushrooms, Pesto, and Sun-Dried Tomatoes

Serves 1

I feel like a magician using pesto in the kitchen—it adds instant flavor, color, and excitement to almost any dish! Here, savory sun-dried tomatoes and mushrooms complement the bright flavor of the pesto.

1 boneless skinless chicken breast

3 Baby Bella or white mushrooms, sliced

1 sun-dried tomato, chopped

1 tablespoon plus 1 teaspoon prepared pesto

1 tablespoon shredded mozzarella cheese

Salt and pepper to taste

1. Preheat oven to 400ºF.

2. Cut a 20" piece of parchment.

3. Line a baking sheet with aluminum foil.

4. Place the chicken on the parchment.

5. Add the other ingredients on top of the chicken so they are spilling over the sides.

6. Fold the parchment.

7. Bake for 20 minutes.

Calories: 272 | Fat: 10 g | Protein: 40 g | Sodium: 211 mg | Carbohydrates: 4 g | Fiber: 1 g

Chicken Paprikash

Serves 1

I turn to this dish when I feel as if I've exhausted everything else in my repertoire. It's warm and comforting and easy to make. For a really exciting flavor, substitute smoked paprika for the regular paprika.

4 ounces fresh, refrigerated angel hair pasta

½ boneless skinless chicken breast, sliced

½ cup canned diced tomato with juice

⅓ cup light sour cream

½ teaspoon paprika

Salt and pepper to taste

¼ teaspoon onion powder

2 teaspoons cornstarch

1 teaspoon olive oil

4 tablespoons chicken broth

1. Preheat oven to 400ºF.
2. Cut a 20" piece of parchment.
3. Line a baking sheet with aluminum foil.
4. Soak the pasta in hot water for about 5 minutes, in a bowl or in your sink.
5. Spray the parchment with cooking spray.
6. Place the pasta on the parchment.
7. Top with the chicken.
8. Mix all the other ingredients together in a small bowl.
9. Pour over the chicken and pasta.
10. Gently stir to ensure the sauce gets down to the pasta.
11. Fold the parchment.
12. Bake for 27 minutes.

Calories: 501 | Fat: 18 g | Protein: 25 g | Sodium: 505 mg | Carbohydrates: 62 g | Fiber: 4 g

Chicken Uncasserole

Serves 1

My favorite chicken casserole is creamy and loaded with spinach and bread—but it's messy. This version cooks up quickly and cleans up even quicker!

1 piece whole wheat bread, ripped into bite-size pieces

2 tablespoons heavy cream

1 tablespoon skim milk

1 tablespoon white wine

½ teaspoon lemon juice

Pinch garlic powder

Pinch onion powder

Salt and pepper to taste

1 boneless skinless chicken breast, cut into bite-size pieces

¼ cup Parmesan cheese

20 baby spinach leaves

2 Triscuit or other wheat crackers

1. Preheat oven to 400ºF.

2. Cut a 20" piece of parchment.

3. Line a baking sheet with aluminum foil.

4. Place the bread in a small bowl and cover with cream, milk, wine, lemon juice, garlic powder, onion powder, salt, and pepper.

5. Allow it to soak for a few minutes.

6. Stir in the chicken.

7. Place this mixture in the center of a piece of parchment.

8. Sprinkle the top with half the cheese.

9. Top with the spinach leaves and then the rest of the cheese.

10. Fold the parchment.

11. Bake for 25 minutes.

12. Open the parchment and crumble the crackers on top.

13. Spray the crumbled crackers with cooking spray and return to the oven to broil for 2 minutes.

Calories: 441 | Fat: 23 g | Protein: 34 g | Sodium: 661 mg | Carbohydrates: 23 g | Fiber: 2 g

Party in a Packet

Serves 4

Ridiculously easy, with flavor that will wow you, this dish puts leftover party snacks to work. It's also a great dinner for when you want something fun. Serving kids a dish called "Party in a Packet" is sure to pique their interest!

4 boneless skinless chicken breasts

Salt and pepper to taste

4 tablespoons prepared French onion dip (found in the dairy case)

1 cup semi-crushed whole-grain cheese crackers (like whole-grain Cheez-It, whole-grain Goldfish, or Late July organic cheese crackers)

1. Preheat oven to 400ºF.
2. Cut four 20" pieces of parchment.
3. Line a baking sheet with aluminum foil.
4. Place one chicken breast in the center of one piece of parchment.
5. Add salt and pepper.
6. Brush 1 tablespoon of the dip over chicken breast.
7. Cover with ¼ cup of the crackers.
8. Repeat for the other packets.
9. Fold the parchment.
10. Bake for 25 minutes.
11. Open the packets and broil for 2–3 minutes.

Calories: 171 | Fat: 7 g | Protein: 21 g | Sodium: 129 mg | Carbohydrates: 5 g | Fiber: 0 g

Raspberry Chicken

Serves 1

Frozen raspberries will work instead of fresh if you can't find fresh or they aren't in season. Serve alongside Rice Pilaf or Couscous with Zucchini Ribbons (both recipes in Chapter 7) for a dish that's bright and cheery in color—and taste!

1 boneless skinless chicken breast

1 tablespoon raspberry vinegar

1 tablespoon olive oil

2 teaspoons raspberry jam

Pinch tarragon

Salt and pepper

10 raspberries, fresh or frozen

1. Place all ingredients except the raspberries in a zip-top bag and mix gently by squishing the bag.
2. Marinate in the refrigerator for at least 20 minutes, up to 4 hours.
3. Preheat oven to 400°F.
4. Cut a 20" piece of parchment.
5. Line a baking sheet with aluminum foil.
6. Place the chicken breast on the parchment.
7. Top with raspberries.
8. Fold the parchment.
9. Bake for 20 minutes.

The marinating instructions for this recipe (and others in the book) are loose. If you can marinate for 4 hours, do so, but if you're pressed for time, even as little as 20 minutes will allow the chicken to take on the flavors of the marinade.

Calories: 325 | Fat: 17 g | Protein: 22 g | Sodium: 55 mg | Carbohydrates: 23 g | Fiber: 8 g

Turkey Enchiladas

Serves 1

Turkey breast and some carrot matchsticks lighten up this dish and make it fun and tasty. Serve with yellow rice and a salad for a complete meal. The recipe makes one enchilada; increase accordingly for the number of people at your table.

1 tortilla (preferably whole wheat)

½ turkey breast fillet, cut into thin strips

⅛ cup canned black beans, drained

⅛ cup grated Cheddar cheese

1 tablespoon light sour cream plus ⅛ cup (reserve the ⅛ cup)

⅛ cup shredded carrots (or matchstick carrots)

¼ cup prepared salsa (choose the hotness you prefer)

1. Preheat oven to 400ºF.
2. Cut a 20" piece of parchment.
3. Line a baking sheet with aluminum foil.
4. Place tortilla on parchment.
5. Cover with all other ingredients except the reserved sour cream and salsa and roll, seam-side down.
6. Top with salsa and ⅛ cup sour cream.
7. Fold parchment.
8. Bake for 30 minutes.

Calories: 305 | Fat: 10 g | Protein: 16 g | Sodium: 346 mg | Carbohydrates: 37 g | Fiber: 5 g

Chicken, Artichoke, and Rice "Casserole"

Serves 1

A casserole minus the messy dish to scrub is a real treat. Artichoke hearts pack a lot of flavor into this savory weeknight favorite. I prefer the frozen hearts to the canned because they aren't soaked in brine and have a cleaner flavor, are easier to work with, and have fewer calories.

½ cup cooked quinoa (or brown rice)

1 boneless skinless chicken breast

Heaping ½ cup frozen artichoke heart quarters, defrosted

1 tablespoon olive oil

⅛ teaspoon sage

⅛ cup chicken broth mixed with 1 teaspoon cornstarch

¼ cup frozen peas

¼ cup canned diced tomatoes

¼ cup Parmesan cheese

Sprinkle of garlic salt

Salt and pepper to taste

1 tablespoon panko bread crumbs

1. Preheat oven to 400°F.
2. Cut a 20" piece of parchment.
3. Line a baking sheet with aluminum foil.
4. Place the rice or quinoa on parchment and top with the chicken.
5. Place the rest of the ingredients except the panko on top.
6. Fold the parchment.
7. Bake for 40 minutes.
8. Open the parchment. Top with panko, and then spray with cooking spray.
9. Broil for 1–2 minutes.

Calories: 500 | Fat: 25 g | Protein: 37 g | Sodium: 730 mg | Carbohydrates: 32 g | Fiber: 6 g

Chicken and Arugula Challah Loaf

Serves 8–10

Fool 'em with this dish, which looks impressive, but comes together incredibly easily. Watch the faces of your guests when they see this come out of the oven, warm, brown, and toasty. When you slice into it, the surprise filling should elicit compliments.

1 large loaf challah bread, whole grain if possible

⅛ pound smoked Gouda, sliced thinly

¼ cup finely chopped onion

2 cups arugula

1 tablespoon Italian seasoning

4 tablespoons light sour cream

Salt and pepper to taste

1 teaspoon cornstarch

1 tablespoon thyme

1 teaspoon dry or powdered mustard

2 boneless skinless chicken breasts, cut into ½" chunks

1. Preheat oven to 400°F.
2. Cut a piece of parchment big enough to encase the entire loaf (about 30").
3. Line a baking sheet with aluminum foil.
4. Slice the top ¼ to ⅓ off the challah loaf, saving this as one whole piece to use as a "lid."
5. From the rest of the loaf, pull out the soft bread inside, leaving a 1" layer around the sides and bottom. You can freeze the parts you remove and save it to make stuffing or bread crumbs at a later date.
6. Layer the smoked Gouda over the sides and bottom, covering as completely as possible. In a medium bowl, mix all other ingredients and chicken together, then place the mixture inside the bread.
7. Cover with the bread "lid."
8. Spray the outside of loaf with cooking spray.
9. Fold the parchment.
10. Bake for 1 hour.
11. Allow it to rest about 5 minutes, then slice to serve.

Challah is a braided egg bread that is slightly sweet. You can also make this recipe using another large loaf of bread, such as Italian or pumpernickel.

Calories: 132 | Fat: 4 g | Protein: 9 g | Sodium: 215 mg | Carbohydrates: 15 g | Fiber: 2 g

Lemon Chicken with Peanut Sauce

Serves 4

Ina Garten (the Barefoot Contessa) taught me the beauty of lemon chicken, which she grills on skewers and serves with a satay sauce. My version works perfectly for parchment paper cooking and delivers a satisfying dish.

For the chicken:

4 boneless skinless chicken breasts

¾ cup lemon juice

¾ cup olive oil

1 tablespoon thyme

Salt and pepper to taste

Zest of 1 lemon

4 scallions

For the peanut sauce:

1 tablespoon olive oil

½ teaspoon onion powder

½ teaspoon garlic powder

½ teaspoon dried ginger

1 tablespoon rice vinegar

Salt and pepper to taste

⅓ cup creamy peanut butter

1 tablespoon lemon juice

1 tablespoon tamari or soy sauce

1½ teaspoons sugar

1. Place all the ingredients except scallions in a zip-top bag and marinate for 20 minutes to 4 hours.

2. Preheat oven to 400°F.

To make peanut sauce:

1. In a glass measuring cup or glass bowl place all of the peanut sauce ingredients.

2. Heat in the microwave for about 30 seconds to a minute until the peanut butter is soft enough that you can mix everything together. It will be a thick paste.

3. Cut four 20" pieces of parchment.

4. Line a baking sheet with aluminum foil.

5. Place one chicken breast on each piece of parchment. Top each breast with ¼ of the peanut sauce.

6. Add the green part of one scallion, cut in quarters, to the top of each packet.

7. Fold the parchment.

8. Bake for 30 minutes.

Calories: 612 | Fat: 53 g | Protein: 26 g | Sodium: 397 mg | Carbohydrates: 11 g | Fiber: 2 g

Chicken Parm Wrap

Serves 1

Chicken Parmesan is a perennial favorite, but it generates a lot of dirty dishes. Here's a healthier version that involves no frying and saves you valuable time in the kitchen.

1 whole wheat tortilla

½ cup spaghetti sauce, divided in half

½ boneless skinless chicken breast (cut horizontally into two pieces)

Salt and pepper to taste

1 tablespoon Italian bread crumbs

1 tablespoon plus 3 tablespoons shredded part-skim mozzarella cheese

1 tablespoon fresh parsley, chopped

1. Preheat oven to 400°F.
2. Cut a 20" piece of parchment.
3. Line a baking sheet with aluminum foil.
4. Place the tortilla on the parchment.
5. Spread ¼ cup spaghetti sauce over the tortilla.
6. Lay the chicken along one side of the tortilla.
7. Season with salt and pepper.
8. Top with bread crumbs and 1 tablespoon cheese.
9. Roll up the tortilla and place seam-side down on the parchment.
10. Top with remaining ¼ cup spaghetti sauce, 3 tablespoons cheese, and parsley.
11. Fold the parchment.
12. Bake for 22 minutes.
13. Open the parchment and broil for 2 minutes.

Calories: 420 | Fat: 16 g | Protein: 25 g | Sodium: 506 mg | Carbohydrates: 44 g | Fiber: 5 g

Hot Cobb "Salad"

Serves 1

I love Cobb salad with all its different flavors that work so well together, so I came up with a hot version of it for a main course. If you don't want to hard-boil your own eggs, you can buy them precooked at the grocery store.

For the salad:

1 cup fresh baby spinach

1 turkey breast fillet

1 slice ham

1 tablespoon prepared guacamole sauce (you can find this refrigerated in the produce section)

½ slice reduced-fat Swiss cheese, cut into strips

1 tablespoon blue cheese

½ slice cooked bacon

½ hard-boiled egg, chopped

2 tablespoons diced tomato

Salt and pepper to taste

Croutons for garnish

For the dressing:

1 teaspoon olive oil

1 teaspoon Dijon mustard

½ teaspoon Worcestershire sauce

½ teaspoon apple cider vinegar

1. Preheat oven to 400°F.
2. Cut a 20" piece of parchment.
3. Line a baking sheet with aluminum foil.
4. Place spinach on parchment.
5. Top with turkey.
6. Place ham on top.
7. Spread guacamole on top.
8. Layer Swiss cheese, blue cheese, bacon, egg, and tomato on top.

To make the dressing:

1. In a small bowl mix together all dressing ingredients.
2. Pour over the ingredients on the parchment.
3. Season with salt and pepper.
4. Fold the parchment.
5. Bake for 15 minutes.
6. Open the packet and top with a few croutons before serving.

Calories: 484 | Fat: 31 g | Protein: 42 g | Sodium: 767 mg | Carbohydrates: 6 g | Fiber: 2 g

Chicken Breast Stuffed with Herbed Goat Cheese

Serves 1

Smooth, creamy goat cheese combines with the vibrancy of fresh herbs to create this spectacular chicken dish. The cheese melts and oozes out of the chicken, making this truly mouthwatering.

1 boneless skinless chicken breast

Salt and pepper to taste

2 ounces goat cheese

1 clove garlic, chopped

½ cup fresh herbs, chopped (use any combination of chives, basil, oregano, thyme, rosemary, sage, or any other herbs you have available) with one sprig reserved

1 tablespoon bread crumbs

1 tablespoon chopped onion

1. Preheat oven to 400°F.
2. Cut a 20" piece of parchment.
3. Line a baking sheet with aluminum foil.
4. Lay the chicken breast on the parchment.
5. Place your hand on top of it.
6. With a knife parallel to your hand, make a slit in one of the long sides of the breast, being careful not to cut all the way through to the other side. Make the slit as deep and as long as possible.
7. Season the chicken with salt and pepper.
8. Mix other ingredients together and stuff it all (reserving about 1 tablespoon) into the slit.
9. It's okay if some of the filling oozes out. Spread the remaining mixture on top of the chicken and top with the sprig of herbs.
10. Fold the parchment.
11. Bake for 15–18 minutes.
12. Open the packet and broil the chicken for about 2 minutes.

Calories: 423 | Fat: 21 g | Protein: 47 g | Sodium: 424 mg | Carbohydrates: 9 g | Fiber: 0.5 g

Chicken Tikka Masala

Serves 1

Savor the warm flavors of India in this "subcontinent in a packet" recipe. Don't let the long list of ingredients scare you off—most are simply herbs and spices that you probably already have in your cupboard.

1 boneless skinless chicken breast

1 tablespoon lemon juice

¼ cup low-fat or nonfat plain yogurt

¼ teaspoon cumin

⅛ teaspoon cinnamon

¼ teaspoon dry ginger

¼ teaspoon salt

1 tablespoon melted butter

1 tablespoon green chili, diced

¼ teaspoon cumin

¼ teaspoon salt

½ cup tomato sauce

1 tablespoon fresh chopped cilantro

1 tablespoon cornstarch

1 tablespoon cream

½ cup cooked brown rice

1. Place chicken, lemon juice, yogurt, cumin, cinnamon, ginger, and salt in a zip-top bag and marinate for 30–60 minutes in the refrigerator.

2. Preheat oven to 400ºF.

3. Cut a 20" piece of parchment.

4. Line a baking sheet with aluminum foil.

5. In a small bowl mix remaining ingredients except rice.

6. Place ½ cup cooked rice on the center of the parchment.

7. Remove chicken from marinade.

8. Place chicken on top of rice.

9. Pour tomato sauce mixture on top.

10. Fold the parchment.

11. Bake for 30 minutes.

Calories: 367 | Fat: 17 g | Protein: 27 g | Sodium: 1043 mg | Carbohydrates: 28 g | Fiber: 3 g

Asian Meatball Sandwiches

Serves 4

Here's an innovative and fun take on a submarine sandwich. I use ground turkey, but you can use lean ground beef if you prefer. Serve with a side of steaming Asian Cabbage (see Chapter 6).

For the meatballs:

1 slice whole wheat bread

1½ tablespoons skim milk

1 teaspoon tamari (or soy sauce)

1 pound ground turkey, 99% fat free

½ of an 8-ounce can of water chestnuts, drained and chopped

3 scallions, chopped

2 cloves garlic, chopped

1 teaspoon fresh ginger, grated

1 egg

¼ cup fresh cilantro, chopped

1½ teaspoons sesame oil

Salt and pepper to taste

For the sub:

4 sandwich or sub rolls (whole wheat if possible), sliced in half

½ cup hoisin sauce

½ cup light mayonnaise

2 tablespoons fresh lemon juice

1. Preheat oven to 350°F.

2. Cut a 20" piece of parchment.

3. Line a baking sheet with aluminum foil.

4. Place the bread and milk in a bowl and allow it to soak for about 5 minutes.

5. Add the other ingredients and mix.

6. Form into 12 meatballs and place on the parchment. Leave uncovered.

7. Bake for 15 minutes.

To prepare the sub:

1. Toast the sub rolls.

2. Mix hoisin, mayonnaise, and lemon juice together in a small bowl and spread on the cut sides of the rolls.

3. Place 3 meatballs on bottom half of each roll and then top with the other half.

Calories: 367 | Fat: 12 g | Protein: 33 g | Sodium: 715 mg | Carbohydrates: 38 g | Fiber: 3 g

Chicken Mole

Serves 1

Looking for something a little unusual for dinner? This recipe fits the bill. The chocolate adds a very subtle smoky flavor, but not a sweetness.

½ cup cooked brown rice

1 boneless skinless chicken breast

Salt and pepper to taste

½ tablespoon butter

¼ ounce unsweetened baking chocolate, chopped (¼ of a square of baking chocolate)

¼ cup Mexican diced tomatoes

⅛ teaspoon chili powder

¼ teaspoon cinnamon

2 tablespoons chicken broth

1. Preheat oven to 400°F.
2. Cut a 20" piece of parchment.
3. Line a baking sheet with aluminum foil.
4. Place rice on parchment.
5. Place chicken on top and season with salt and pepper.
6. Melt butter and chocolate in a small glass bowl in the microwave for about 20 seconds.
7. Stir until the chocolate is completely melted.
8. Place the tomatoes on the chicken; top with chili powder, cinnamon, and chicken broth.
9. Top with chocolate mixture.
10. Fold the parchment.
11. Bake for 25 minutes.

Mole is a traditional Mexican dish that uses unsweetened chocolate. Because it is not sweet, it adds an interesting depth of flavor to the dish. Mexican tomatoes can be found in the canned tomato section of your store. They might be called "tomatoes with cilantro and lime." "Chili tomatoes" are a substitute you can use.

Calories: 310 | Fat: 12 g | Protein: 23 g | Sodium: 253 mg | Carbohydrates: 13 g | Fiber: 3 g

Chicken, Arugula, and Fontina Quesadilla

Serves 2

Who says a quesadilla has to have Mexican flavors? Try making this with deli turkey, spinach, and Swiss cheese. Add any fresh herbs you have on hand.

2 whole wheat tortillas

¾ cup arugula

¾ cup shredded cooked chicken (rotisserie or leftover)

¾ cup shredded fontina cheese

Salt and pepper to taste

2 pinches dry mustard

⅛ teaspoon garlic powder

1. Preheat oven to 400°F.

2. Cut a 20" piece of parchment.

3. Line a baking sheet with aluminum foil.

4. Spray the bottom of a tortilla with cooking spray and place it on the parchment.

5. Spread the arugula over the tortilla and top with the chicken and cheese.

6. Season with salt and pepper and sprinkle with the dry mustard and garlic powder.

7. Place the second tortilla on top and spray with cooking spray.

8. Fold the parchment.

9. Bake for 12–15 minutes, until the cheese is melted.

10. Use a pizza cutter to cut into quarters.

Calories: 398 | Fat: 21 g | Protein: 31 g | Sodium: 596 mg | Carbohydrates: 19 g | Fiber: 1.5 g

Turkey with Tarragon, Rosemary, and Cranberry

Serves 1

For when you're in the mood for the flavors of Thanksgiving without all the fuss, this dish satisfies. Enjoy it alongside mashed potatoes (which you can buy prepared or make your own) or some stuffing. Just like holiday leftovers, this tastes great cold on a sandwich.

1 turkey cutlet

¼ teaspoon tarragon

¼ teaspoon rosemary

2 tablespoons prepared cranberry sauce

1 teaspoon reduced-sodium chicken broth

⅛ teaspoon onion powder

1 tablespoon white wine

Salt and pepper to taste

1. Preheat oven to 400°F.

2. Cut a 20" piece of parchment.

3. Line a baking sheet with aluminum foil.

4. Place the turkey cutlet on the parchment.

5. Place all the other ingredients in a small glass bowl and microwave about 20–30 seconds, then stir to combine. Pour the mixture over the turkey.

6. Fold the parchment.

7. Bake for 10 minutes. Note that these cook extremely quickly because they are very thin and very lean—overcook it and you get shoe leather!

Calories: 102 | Fat: 0.5 g | Protein: 8 g | Sodium: 573 mg | Carbohydrates: 17 g | Fiber: 0.5 g

Buffalo Chicken Wrap

Serves 4

Since I'm from Buffalo, here's a shout-out to my hometown cuisine. This tastes just like the Buffalo wings that are a favorite in my town—and now around the rest of the country, too—but without all the calories.

8 whole wheat tortillas

1 cup light blue cheese dressing, plus more for serving

1 pound ground chicken

1 tablespoon melted butter

¼ cup Frank's hot sauce, plus more for serving

1 rib celery, chopped

½ cup bread crumbs

1 egg

Celery (1 rib plus additional for serving)

1. Preheat oven to 400°F.

2. Cut a 20" piece of parchment.

3. Line a baking sheet with aluminum foil.

4. Lay out the tortillas and spread each with 2 tablespoons of dressing.

5. Mix remaining ingredients except for celery together in a bowl.

6. Place ½ cup of chicken mixture along one side of each tortilla and press to flatten, covering about ¼ of the tortilla.

7. Roll up tortilla and place seam-side down on the parchment.

8. Place two wraps in each piece of parchment.

9. Using a vegetable peeler, peel off the dark green strings on the outside of celery rib and discard. Then use the peeler to create 4 long peels of celery to lay across the top of each wrap.

10. Fold the parchment.

11. Bake for 20 minutes. Serve with additional hot sauce, blue cheese dressing, and celery cut into stalks. Enjoy hot or cold.

Buffalo wings originated at the Anchor Bar restaurant in downtown Buffalo in 1964. Teresa Bellissimo needed to whip up a snack to feed her son's hungry friends late one night in the restaurant. Buffalo wings were the result. They're now one of the most popular takeout foods in the country.

Calories: 399 | Fat: 9.5 g | Protein: 36 g | Sodium: 737 mg | Carbohydrates: 32 g | Fiber: 5 g

Chicken Adobo

Serves 1

This dish originated in the Philippines and begs to be served with rice and steamed vegetables. Don't forget to discard the bay leaf after cooking!

1 boneless skinless chicken breast

1 bay leaf

Salt and pepper to taste

1 small clove garlic, chopped

¼ cup coconut cream (canned)

1 teaspoon tamari sauce (or soy sauce)

1 teaspoon rice wine vinegar

1. Preheat the oven to 400ºF.
2. Cut a 20" piece of parchment.
3. Line a baking sheet with aluminum foil.
4. Place the chicken breast on parchment.
5. Top with the bay leaf and season with salt and pepper.
6. Add the garlic.
7. Pour the coconut cream, tamari, and rice wine vinegar over the top.
8. Fold the parchment.
9. Bake for 15–20 minutes.

Coconut cream is similar to coconut milk, but is thicker and pastier. Note that it is *not* the same as cream of coconut, which is sweetened and used in beverages like piña coladas.

Calories: 264 | Fat: 16 g | Protein: 24 g | Sodium: 419 mg | Carbohydrates: 9.5 g | Fiber: 2 g

Stuffed Chicken Breast

Serves 1

I love this method of hiding a filling inside a chicken breast. Nuts are the surprise ingredient in this dish. You can substitute prosciutto for the ham if you have some you want to use up.

1 boneless skinless chicken breast

1 tablespoon chopped pecans or walnuts, plus ½ teaspoon (reserved)

1 small clove garlic, chopped

1 teaspoon olive oil

1 tablespoon chopped ham

1 tablespoon bread crumbs

2 teaspoons reduced-sodium chicken broth plus 1 tablespoon (reserved)

Salt and pepper to taste

1 tablespoon fresh parsley, chopped

Pinch of thyme

1 tablespoon white wine

1 teaspoon Dijon mustard

1 teaspoon cornstarch

1. Preheat oven to 400°F.

2. Cut a 20" piece of parchment.

3. Line a baking sheet with aluminum foil.

4. Lay the chicken breast on the parchment. Place your hand on top of it.

5. With a knife parallel to your hand, make a slit in one of the long sides of the breast, being careful not to cut all the way through to the other side. Make the slit as deep and as long as possible.

6. In a medium glass bowl place 1 tablespoon nuts, the garlic, and the oil and microwave on high for 30 seconds. To that bowl mix in the ham, bread crumbs, 2 teaspoons of the chicken broth, salt, pepper, parsley, and thyme.

7. Stuff mixture into the pocket in the chicken. Lay the chicken on the parchment.

8. In a small bowl mix remaining tablespoon of chicken broth, wine, cornstarch, and Dijon. Pour over chicken.

9. Fold the parchment.

10. Bake for 20 minutes.

11. Open the packet and sprinkle the reserved nuts on top before serving.

Calories: 261 | Fat: 12 g | Protein: 25 g | Sodium: 345 mg | Carbohydrates: 10 g | Fiber: 1 g

Lettuce-Wrapped Chicken

Serves 4–6

The Asian-flavored chicken filling for this fun dish comes out of the oven slightly solid so it holds together well once inside the lettuce wrapping. Just scoop off a portion and place on the lettuce leaves—everyone will enjoy assembling their own wraps! Serve alongside brown rice.

1 pound ground chicken

½ of a 10-ounce package of mushrooms (white or Baby Bella), chopped

1 8-ounce can water chestnuts, drained and chopped

2 scallions, chopped

Salt and pepper to taste

1 small onion, chopped

1 large clove garlic, chopped

1 tablespoon brown sugar

2 tablespoons rice wine vinegar

1 tablespoon ketchup

1 tablespoon lemon juice

2 tablespoons cornstarch

1 tablespoon chili paste (this is found in the Asian section of the grocery store)

3 tablespoons tamari or soy sauce

1 teaspoon sesame oil

1 head Boston lettuce, broken down into individual leaves

1. Preheat oven to 400ºF.

2. Cut a 20" piece of parchment.

3. Place foil on baking sheet, then the parchment.

4. In a large bowl, combine all ingredients except the lettuce. Stir well.

5. Place chicken mixture on the parchment, forming a round or rectangular loaf, of even thickness throughout.

6. Fold the parchment. Make sure it is sealed tightly.

7. Bake for 50 minutes.

8. Serve with lettuce. Place a scoop of filling in the leaf, fold up like a taco, and eat with your hands.

Calories: 128 | Fat: 4 g | Protein: 13 g | Sodium: 470 mg | Carbohydrates: 8.5 g | Fiber: 1 g

Chicken Tetrazzini Roll-Ups

Serves 1

Instead of the traditional spaghetti, this recipe uses fresh lasagna sheets, which you can find in the refrigerated section of the market. They don't have the ridges along the side that regular lasagna noodles have, but they work well for rolling up a filling.

1 sheet fresh refrigerated lasagna

½ boneless skinless chicken breast, cut into 1" pieces

3 white or Baby Bella mushrooms, sliced

2 tablespoons cream, plus 1 teaspoon (reserved)

⅛ teaspoon paprika, plus a pinch

Salt and pepper to taste

¼ teaspoon onion powder (divided use)

2 tablespoons skim milk

3 tablespoons chicken broth

4 tablespoons light sour cream

2 tablespoons cooking sherry

⅛ teaspoon garlic powder

1 tablespoon cornstarch

2 tablespoons grated Parmesan cheese

1 sprig fresh parsley

1. Preheat oven to 400°F.
2. Cut a 20" piece of parchment.
3. Line a baking sheet with aluminum foil.
4. Lay lasagna sheet on parchment.
5. Place chicken on a short end of the sheet.
6. Add half the mushrooms.
7. Drizzle the 2 tablespoons of cream.
8. Add a pinch of paprika, salt, pepper, and ⅛ teaspoon onion powder.
9. Roll the sheet up and place it seam-side down on the parchment.
10. In a small bowl mix remaining cream, milk, chicken broth, sour cream, sherry, garlic powder, cornstarch, ⅛ teaspoon paprika, ⅛ teaspoon onion powder, salt, pepper, and the remaining mushrooms.
11. Spoon over the roll.
12. Sprinkle cheese on top and add a sprig of parsley.
13. Fold the parchment.
14. Bake for 20 minutes.

Calories: 421 | Fat: 17 g | Protein: 27 g | Sodium: 388 mg | Carbohydrates: 40 g | Fiber: 2 g

Upside-Down Chicken "No-Pot" Pie

Serves 2

Mmm. Potpie. The ultimate comfort food. This has all the flavors of traditional chicken potpie with none of the mess. If you have leftover cooked vegetables, you can substitute them for the peas and carrots.

1 refrigerated unbaked pie crust

¾ cup shredded or cubed cooked chicken (rotisserie or leftover)

¼ cup frozen peas

5 baby carrots, thinly sliced, then chopped

1 heaping tablespoon chopped onion

2 tablespoons cream

4 tablespoons butter

2 tablespoons skim milk

2 teaspoons cornstarch

2 tablespoons Parmesan cheese, plus 1 tablespoon (reserved)

Salt and pepper to taste

1. Preheat oven to 400°F.

2. Cut a 20" piece of parchment.

3. Line a baking sheet with aluminum foil.

4. Place the crust on the parchment.

5. Squish up the edges to form a 6" × 6" or 7" × 7" square, pinching the crust so it stands up and forms a bit of a barrier.

6. Sprinkle the chicken on top of the crust and add peas, carrots, and onion.

7. In a medium glass bowl, mix the cream, butter, milk, cornstarch, and 2 tablespoons Parmesan cheese. Microwave for about 20 seconds then stir until the butter is melted and the mixture is thickened.

8. Add salt and pepper.

9. Spoon the sauce over the chicken and vegetables.

10. Top with remaining Parmesan.

11. Fold the parchment.

12. Bake for 20 minutes.

Calories: 695 | Fat: 50 g | Protein: 16 g | Sodium: 778 mg | Carbohydrates: 44 g | Fiber: 3 g

CHAPTER 3

Pork and Lamb Dishes

People often think ham, lamb, or pork dishes require a lot of work, but this section will proves that's not the case. Luscious ribs, tasty lamb, flavorful sausage, and tender ham dishes work wonderfully well cooked in parchment. Ham especially lends itself to parchment because it has so much flavor and comes already cooked. These recipes give you great results to put on your table.

Carol's Crazy Hot Ham Sandwiches

Serves 4

My husband grew up eating ham sandwiches that his mother baked in the oven (with four kids, grilling them stovetop was not feasible), so I've built on her idea in this recipe. When you make the Roasted Parmesan Broccoli and Cauliflower (see Chapter 6), make a little extra broccoli and save it for these sandwiches. This sandwich pairs perfectly with veggies and dip.

Honey mustard

8 slices rye bread

Sweet chipotle sauce

8 slices ham

4 slices reduced-fat Swiss or Gruyère cheese

1 large or 2 small tomatoes (8 slices total)

1 cup cooked broccoli

> Feel free to make substitutions in this recipe. If you don't like rye, try pumpernickel or sourdough bread. Swap out the Swiss cheese for provolone or Cheddar. Or try using horseradish mustard for some fire. You can also use turkey instead of ham if you prefer.

1. Preheat oven to 400°F.
2. Cut four 15" pieces of parchment.
3. Spread as much mustard on four slices of bread as suits your taste.
4. Spread as much sweet chipotle sauce on the other four pieces of bread as you like. Working with four slices of bread, place two slices of ham and one slice of cheese on each piece of bread.
5. Remove the seeds and liquid from tomato slices and place the tomatoes on a paper towel to drain for about 3 minutes.
6. Add 2 slices of tomato to each sandwich. Break the broccoli up into smaller floret pieces and lay them across the sandwiches. Top with the chipotle-covered bread.
7. Spray both exterior sides of the sandwiches with cooking spray.
8. Wrap each sandwich individually in a piece of parchment. Make sure the packets are sealed tightly and then wrap in foil.
9. Set the sandwiches directly on the oven racks (placing them on a tray will cause the side facing down to get mushy) in the middle of the oven.
10. Bake for 15 minutes.

Calories: 482 | Fat: 25 g | Protein: 25 g | Sodium: 533 mg | Carbohydrates: 44 g | Fiber: 9 g

Luscious Ribs

Serves 2

I love ribs, but boy do they make a big mess! This method keeps everything inside the parchment for easy cleanup and creates moist, tender ribs you won't be able to get enough of! If you prefer, you can use a prepared barbecue sauce for the second part of this recipe.

For the ribs:

1 tablespoon soy sauce

1 tablespoon molasses

1 tablespoon brown sugar

Salt and pepper to taste

¼ teaspoon garlic powder

1 rack baby back ribs, cut in half

For the sauce:

½ cup ketchup

2 teaspoons yellow mustard

2 teaspoons cider vinegar

¼ teaspoon garlic salt

2 tablespoons brown sugar

1. Mix all ingredients except ribs in a zip-top bag. Add the ribs to the marinade and refrigerate 20 minutes to 4 hours (the longer you marinate the ribs, the more flavor you'll get).

2. Preheat oven to 400°F.

3. Line a baking sheet with foil. Cut a 24" piece of parchment and the same size piece of foil. Lay the parchment on top of the piece of foil. Place the ribs on top of the layered parchment and foil.

4. Pour the marinade over the ribs. Fold the parchment tightly.

5. Carefully overwrap the package in the outer foil, being sure to seal up any seams. Bake for 2 hours. Remove from oven, and carefully open up the packet.

To make barbeque sauce:

1. In a small bowl, mix together barbecue sauce ingredients.

2. Brush ribs with about half the sauce (reserving the rest to serve with the ribs on the side).

3. Cut away excess parchment and foil.

4. Reduce oven temperature to 350°F and bake for 20 minutes.

Calories: 653 | Fat: 32 g | Protein: 29 g | Sodium: 1067 mg | Carbohydrates: 69 g | Fiber: 2.5 g

Pork Chop with Birch and Kale

Serves 1

Readers of my blog love this recipe, a warming winter dish. If you've ever scratched your head and wondered how to cook kale, here's an easy solution. The birch syrup adds an unexpected twist!

1 bone-in pork chop

Salt and pepper to taste

1 tablespoon birch syrup

½ teaspoon country-style Dijon mustard (or other grainy mustard)

½ small clove garlic, chopped

Large handful kale, stems removed

1. Preheat oven to 400ºF.
2. Cut a 20" piece of parchment.
3. Line a baking sheet with aluminum foil.
4. Place the pork chop on the parchment paper.
5. Season with salt and pepper.
6. Drizzle the birch syrup on top.
7. Drop the mustard and garlic on top.
8. Using a spoon or knife, rub the chop with the ingredients.
9. Flip chop over, smearing with sauce from the packet, then turn it back to the first side.
10. Top with the kale.
11. Fold the parchment.
12. Bake for 30 minutes.

Birch syrup is similar to maple syrup, but it's thinner and less sweet. It has a woodsy, almost smoky flavor and is not as cloying as maple syrup. You can buy it online at *www.AlaskaBirch Syrup.com* or *www.AlaskaSyrup .com* if you can't find it locally.

Calories: 462 | Fat: 13 g | Protein: 41 g | Sodium: 1521 mg | Carbohydrates: 43 g | Fiber: 2.5 g

Greek Lamb Meatball Pitas

Serves 4

Delicious for lunch or dinner, these pita pockets feature whole-grain bulgur (found near the rice in your grocery store), which cooks quickly in the microwave and gives the lamb meatballs a light texture. Serve some fresh fruit with this to complete the meal.

1 pound ground lamb

½ cup cooked bulgur, cooked according to package instructions

Salt and pepper to taste

⅛ cup onion, chopped

1 clove garlic, chopped

1 egg

2 tablespoons fresh mint, chopped

1 teaspoon Greek seasoning (or oregano)

¼ cup fat-free feta cheese, plus more for serving

4 whole wheat pitas

1 cup low-fat (or nonfat) plain regular or Greek yogurt

1 tablespoon lemon juice

1 teaspoon salt

1 small cucumber, chopped

Lettuce

Tomato

1. Preheat oven to 400°F.

2. Cut a 20" piece of parchment.

3. Line a baking sheet with aluminum foil.

4. In a bowl, mix lamb, cooked bulgur, salt, pepper, onion, garlic, egg, mint, Greek seasoning, and ¼ cup feta.

5. Form into 12 meatballs.

6. Place on parchment. Leave uncovered.

7. Bake for 20 minutes.

8. Warm the pitas.

9. In a small bowl mix yogurt, lemon juice, salt, and cucumber.

10. Set out the meatballs, pitas, yogurt sauce, lettuce, tomato, and additional feta so that each person can assemble his or her own pita.

Calories: 462 | Fat: 13 g | Protein: 41 g | Sodium: 1571 mg | Carbohydrates: 43 g | Fiber: 2.5 g

Pork Chops with Fruity Sauce

Serves 1

I naturally think of pork chops as a wonderful fall and winter dish, but the fruit flavor in this reminds me that summer eventually comes! Play with this and test out different types of jam. I've made it with passion fruit jelly with out-of-this-world results.

½ cup cooked brown rice

1 bone-in pork chop

1 tablespoon peach jam or orange marmalade

¼ teaspoon Dijon mustard

½ teaspoon soy sauce

¼ teaspoon lemon juice

1 tablespoon chicken broth

Pinch of ground cloves

Salt and pepper to taste

1. Preheat oven to 400°F.
2. Cut a 20" piece of parchment.
3. Line a baking sheet with aluminum foil.
4. Place the rice on parchment and cover with pork chop.
5. Drop jam/marmalade, mustard, soy, lemon juice, and broth on top of the chop and spread with a spoon.
6. Sprinkle with cloves, salt, and pepper.
7. Fold the parchment.
8. Bake for 30 minutes.

Calories: 296 | Fat: 9 g | Protein: 19 g | Sodium: 249 mg | Carbohydrates: 19 g | Fiber: 0.5 g

Ham Loaf

Serves 6

A cross between meatloaf and sausage, ham loaf works sliced on a sandwich, pan-fried the next day, or as a main course. Add half a can of chopped pineapple to this to make it taste fruity!

⅓ pound deli ham

½ cup ground pork

¼ cup seasoned breadcrumbs

1 egg

⅓ cup shredded Cheddar cheese, plus extra for topping

¼ cup light cream cheese

3 ounces Swiss cheese (from a wedge)

¼ cup cooked brown rice

Salt and pepper to taste

2 teaspoons stone-ground mustard (you can use yellow mustard or Dijon as substitutes)

¼ teaspoon onion powder

¼ cup sweet and sour sauce

1. Preheat oven to 400°F.
2. Cut a 24" piece of parchment.
3. Line a baking sheet with aluminum foil.
4. Place all ingredients in a food processor and process until completely ground and mixed, like ground meat.
5. If you do not have a food processor, dice the ham and Swiss cheese and mix all ingredients together in a bowl.
6. Place the mixture on parchment paper and form into a 9" loaf.
7. Top with a sprinkle of additional Cheddar cheese.
8. Fold the parchment.
9. Bake for 30 minutes.

Calories: 254 | Fat: 15 g | Protein: 17 g | Sodium: 555 mg | Carbohydrates: 8 g | Fiber: 1 g

Molasses-Glazed Pork Chops

Serves 1

Molasses gives this dish some depth and brings out the heartiness of the pork chops. I like to use blackstrap molasses, but any will work. Serve with a loaf of crusty bread and some green beans for a filling dinner.

1 bone-in pork chop

1 teaspoon molasses

½ teaspoon soy sauce

½ teaspoon fresh grated ginger

⅛ teaspoon garlic powder

1. Preheat oven to 400°F.
2. Cut a 20" piece of parchment.
3. Line a baking sheet with aluminum foil.
4. Place the chop on the parchment.
5. Place the other ingredients on top of the chop and spread them around with a spoon.
6. Flip the chop over once and then again to distribute the sauce on both sides.
7. Fold the parchment.
8. Bake for 30 minutes.

Calories: 181 | Fat: 9 g | Protein: 18 g | Sodium: 206 mg | Carbohydrates: 6 g | Fiber: 0 g

Minty Lamb Chops

Serves 4

Fresh mint, garlic, and bread crumbs make a tasty topping to lamb chops. They look so pretty nestled in the middle of the parchment paper. If you prefer your lamb very rare, reduce the cooking time by about 5 minutes.

4 lamb chops

2 cloves garlic, chopped

2 tablespoons chopped onion

1 teaspoon white vinegar

Salt and pepper to taste

½ piece of whole wheat bread, shredded into small pieces

1 tablespoon melted butter

Leaves from 1 bunch fresh mint, chopped

1. Preheat oven to 400°F.
2. Cut a 30" piece of parchment.
3. Line a baking sheet with aluminum foil.
4. Place the chops together on the parchment.
5. Combine all other ingredients in a small bowl.
6. Spread the mixture on top of the lamb.
7. Fold the parchment.
8. Bake for 40 minutes.
9. Open the parchment and broil for 3–4 minutes, until the top begins to brown.

If you have a mini food processor, put all the ingredients except the lamb in it (unchopped) and pulse to make the topping in a jiffy.

Calories: 189 | Fat: 9 g | Protein: 22 g | Sodium: 98 mg | Carbohydrates: 2 g | Fiber: 0 g

Pork Chops with Applesauce

Serves 1

Pork and apples go together like bread and butter—and cooking the pork chops with applesauce combines the flavors in every bite. Sage and cinnamon heighten the flavor.

1 bone-in pork chop

1 cup applesauce

1 clove garlic, chopped

1 teaspoon apple cider vinegar

⅛ teaspoon sage (or ¼ teaspoon fresh, chopped)

⅛ teaspoon cinnamon plus a pinch (reserved)

½ teaspoon Worcestershire sauce

Salt and pepper to taste

1 paper-thin slice of apple, cut from a cored apple

1. Preheat oven to 400ºF.

2. Cut a 20" piece of parchment.

3. Line a baking sheet with aluminum foil.

4. Place the pork chop on the parchment.

5. Add applesauce, garlic, vinegar, sage, ⅛ teaspoon cinnamon, Worcestershire sauce, salt, and pepper on top of the pork chop.

6. Place the thin apple slice on top and sprinkle with cinnamon.

7. Fold the parchment.

8. Bake for 30 minutes.

Calories: 384 | Fat: 20 g | Protein: 20 g | Sodium: 80 mg | Carbohydrates: 28 g | Fiber: 4 g

Ham Steak with Pineapple Rice

Serves 1 or 2

Ham steaks are really just thick slices of ham. If you have a leftover ham from a holiday dinner, simply slice off a 1" thick piece to use in this recipe. The pineapple rice dresses it all up!

1 ham steak

½ cup cooked brown rice

1 teaspoon brown sugar

1 teaspoon soy sauce

¼ cup pineapple pieces

⅛ cup pineapple juice

1 teaspoon cornstarch

1. Preheat oven to 400°F.

2. Cut a 20" piece of parchment.

3. Line a baking sheet with aluminum foil.

4. Place the ham steak on the parchment.

5. In a small bowl, mix remaining ingredients. Spoon on top of the ham.

6. Fold the parchment.

7. Bake for 13 minutes.

Calories: 311 | Fat: 4 g | Protein: 19 g | Sodium: 945 mg | Carbohydrates: 21 g | Fiber: 1.5 g

Chorizo with Polenta and Broccolini

Serves 4

Broccolini tastes familiar because it's from the same vegetable family as broccoli, but it's more refined. This wildly flavorful dish serves as a complete meal; no need to cook anything else tonight!

1 pound premade polenta, low-fat if possible

1 pound chorizo (spicy pork sausage)

½ pound broccolini (1 medium bunch)

14-ounce can diced tomatoes

4 ounces feta cheese or *queso fresco*

½ teaspoon chili powder

Salt and pepper to taste

This recipe calls for a tube of premade polenta, which is sold in the produce section at your grocery store. You can also make your own polenta in your rice cooker or in your microwave by following the instructions on the package. Place 1½ cup of freshly cooked polenta on each piece of parchment instead of using sliced polenta. If you made your own, season it with some onion and garlic powder. If you don't like chorizo, try Italian, Polish, or spiced turkey sausage in this dish.

1. Preheat oven to 400°F.

2. Cut four 20" pieces of parchment.

3. Line a baking sheet with aluminum foil.

4. Slice eight 1" rounds of polenta, two per person and per packet, and place them on the parchment paper.

5. Divide the chorizo into four equal sections. Place one piece on each serving of polenta.

6. Top each with two stalks of broccolini, crowns facing opposite ends.

7. Place ¼ of the tomatoes on top of each and sprinkle with ¼ of the cheese.

8. Divide ½ teaspoon chili powder among the packets and season with salt and pepper to taste.

9. Fold the parchment.

10. Bake for 30 minutes.

Calories: 826 | Fat: 50 g | Protein: 38 g | Sodium: 2206 mg | Carbohydrates: 53 g | Fiber: 6 g

Pork Chops with Sauerkraut and Apple

Serves 4

This dish smells phenomenal as it bakes. I'm a big fan of sauerkraut, which although tangy, isn't too sour when paired with the pork in this dish. Even if you think you don't care for it, I urge you to give this a try!

4 boneless pork chops

¼ teaspoon garlic powder

Salt and pepper to taste

2 teaspoons olive oil

4 ounces jarred or canned sauerkraut (you can also buy it fresh, in a bag)

1 apple, cored and thinly sliced

4 teaspoons brown sugar

A pinch or two of caraway seeds

1. Preheat oven to 400°F.
2. Cut four 20" pieces of parchment.
3. Line a baking sheet with aluminum foil.
4. Place one pork chop in the center of each piece of parchment.
5. Sprinkle ¼ of the garlic powder (¹⁄₁₆ teaspoon) over it.
6. Season with salt and pepper.
7. Drizzle ½ teaspoon olive oil on top.
8. Top with ¼ of sauerkraut.
9. Arrange ¼ of the apple over and around it.
10. Sprinkle contents in the packet with 1 teaspoon brown sugar and a small pinch of caraway seeds.
11. Repeat for other 3 chops.
12. Fold the parchment.
13. Bake for 20 minutes.

Sauerkraut is a traditional German dish, made up of fermented (or pickled) cabbage. It has a wonderful sour flavor that complements pork especially well.

Calories: 210 | Fat: 9 g | Protein: 23 g | Sodium: 128 mg | Carbohydrates: 8 g | Fiber: 1.5 g

Ham and Asparagus Crepes

Serves 1

You can normally find prepared crepes in the refrigerated produce section of the grocery store. I've made this for a holiday brunch, to rave reviews. It's also nice for a quick dinner, and the crepe disguises the asparagus so your kids might eat it! This makes 1–2 crepes per person, depending on what else you are serving.

1 crepe

1 tablespoon chive and onion cream cheese

½ teaspoon Dijon mustard

1 tablespoon shredded reduced-fat Swiss cheese

2 slices deli ham

5 asparagus spears, bottoms trimmed

1. Preheat oven to 400°F.

2. Cut a 20" piece of parchment.

3. Line a baking sheet with aluminum foil.

4. Place crepe on the parchment.

5. Spread the cream cheese and then the Dijon on the crepe, covering as much as possible (you won't have enough to cover the entire thing).

6. Sprinkle the Swiss cheese on top.

7. Lay the ham down to cover as much of the crepe as possible.

8. Place asparagus spears together at one side of the crepe and roll it up from that side.

9. Place seam-side down on the parchment.

10. Repeat, making as many crepes as you want and placing them side by side in the parchment.

11. Fold the parchment.

12. Bake for 20 minutes.

Calories: 317 | Fat: 20 g | Protein: 14 g | Sodium: 832 mg | Carbohydrates: 19 g | Fiber: 2 g

Haleiwa Sandwich

Serves 1

The best sandwich I ever ate was at a tiny organic café in Haleiwa on the north shore of Oahu, in Hawaii. Every time I make this, it takes me back—but then I really crave a "shave" ice for dessert!

1 onion roll or whole wheat roll, sliced in half

Honey mustard

Light mayonnaise of your choice

2 slices ripe tomato

½ avocado, sliced

2 slices organic bacon, cooked in the microwave

¼ cup sprouts, any kind you like

1 slice reduced-fat Swiss cheese

1. Preheat oven to 400°F.
2. Cut a 20" piece of parchment.
3. Line a baking sheet with aluminum foil.
4. Place the roll on the parchment.
5. Put honey mustard on one half and light Miracle Whip on the other.
6. Remove the seeds from the tomato slices, and then lay the tomatoes on a paper towel that has been folded in half. Let set for about 3 minutes.
7. Blot the top of the tomatoes with another paper towel.
8. Lay the tomatoes on the sandwich bottom.
9. Top with avocado, bacon, and then the sprouts.
10. Place the cheese on top.
11. Fold the parchment.
12. Bake for 15 minutes, until cheese is melted.

Calories: 401 | Fat: 27 g | Protein: 21 g | Sodium: 608 mg | Carbohydrates: 23 g | Fiber: 7 g

Pork Chops with Pumpkin and Cream

Serves 1

If you're longing for fall comfort food, this fits the bill. Pork, together with pumpkin, herbs, and spices, smells heavenly while baking, and the end result is moist and flavorful. Don't use pumpkin pie filling for this recipe or you're in for an awfully sweet entrée!

1 boneless pork chop

¼ cup canned unsweetened pumpkin

⅛ teaspoon onion powder

⅛ teaspoon garlic powder

⅛ teaspoon dried sage

⅛ teaspoon cinnamon

Salt and pepper to taste

Pinch of ground cloves

1 tablespoon heavy cream

1 sage leaf

1. Preheat the oven to 400°F.

2. Cut a 20" piece of parchment.

3. Line a baking sheet with aluminum foil.

4. Place the pork chop on the parchment.

5. In a small bowl, mix all the remaining ingredients except the sage leaf.

6. Pour the mixture over the pork, and top with sage leaf.

7. Fold the parchment.

8. Bake for 20 minutes.

Calories: 277 | Fat: 19 g | Protein: 23 g | Sodium: 40 mg | Carbohydrates: 2.5 g | Fiber: 0.5 g

Sausage-Stuffed Tomatoes

Serves 1

This recipe helps use up your late summer bumper crop of tomatoes! The fresher and riper your tomatoes, the more delicious the dish. Make one per person as a side dish or two if you want to enjoy as a main dish.

1 large ripe tomato

½ piece whole wheat bread, ripped into small pieces

½ teaspoon Italian seasoning

½ teaspoon olive oil

Salt and pepper to taste

2 tablespoons shredded part-skim mozzarella cheese

2 tablespoons Italian sausage, removed from the casing

¼ teaspoon garlic powder

1. Preheat oven to 400°F.
2. Cut a 20" piece of parchment.
3. Line a baking sheet with aluminum foil.
4. Cut the top off the tomato; set aside to use as a "lid." Remove any stem.
5. Scoop out the inside of the tomato, reserving the pulp and discarding the seeds and juice.
6. Chop 1 tablespoon of the pulp.
7. In a small bowl mix the pulp, bread, Italian seasoning, olive oil, salt, pepper, mozzarella, sausage, and garlic powder.
8. Place the tomato on the parchment.
9. Fill with the stuffing and top with the tomato "lid."
10. Fold the parchment.
11. Bake for 25 minutes.

Calories: 130 | Fat: 6.5 g | Protein: 7 g | Sodium: 171 mg | Carbohydrates: 12 g | Fiber: 2 g

CHAPTER 4

Beef and Veal Dishes

This section offers some unique ways to cook beef in parchment. I try to always cook with organic, grass-fed beef when I can get it, and hope you'll try it too! Beef might not be something you automatically think of when you consider parchment paper cooking, but it works well when paired with sauces and vegetables.

Steak and Shrooms

Serves 4

Steak and mushrooms make a hearty meal that pairs well with German Potatoes (see Chapter 7) or with garlic bread. Or try whipping up the Roasted Carrots, Parsnip, and Rutabaga with Birch Syrup (see Chapter 6) to serve alongside. Be sure to spoon out a little sauce with your meat and mushrooms if you are plating this up—the sauce is the best part!

1 pound strip steaks (preferably four ¼-pound pieces)

12 Baby Bella mushrooms (you can use white mushrooms if you prefer)

Sea salt to taste

Pepper to taste

4 teaspoons Worcestershire sauce

4 teaspoons steak sauce

1 teaspoon hoisin sauce

1. Preheat oven to 400°F.

2. Cut a 20" piece of parchment.

3. Line a baking sheet with aluminum foil.

4. Trim the fat and gristle off the steaks.

5. Slice the steak into ¼" slices, so that they look like thick matchsticks. My grocery store sells very thin strip steaks of about ¼ pound each and that is what I use for this recipe. If you buy thicker strip steaks, just be sure to cut your slices in half lengthwise to get that matchstick appearance.

6. Wash the mushrooms. Slice thinly.

7. Place the mushrooms on the parchment and cover them with the steak.

8. Sprinkle with sea salt and pepper.

9. Mix Worcestershire, steak sauce, and hoisin in a small bowl.

10. Using a spoon, drizzle this mixture evenly over the entire dish.

11. Fold the parchment.

12. Bake for 15 minutes.

Calories: 236 | Fat: 8 g | Protein: 36 g | Sodium: 155 mg | Carbohydrates: 3 g | Fiber: 0.5 g

St. Patrick's Day Sandwich

Serves 1

While perfectly suited for St. Patrick's Day dinner leftovers, you can make this any time of year. If you made your own corned beef and cabbage, use the cooked cabbage from that dish in this sandwich. Otherwise, prepared sauerkraut does the trick.

Dijon mustard to taste

2 slices rye bread

Ketchup to taste

Horseradish sauce to taste

Corned beef (a nice thick slice if you're using home-cooked corned beef, or 4 deli slices)

Cooked cabbage leaf or ¼ cup sauerkraut

1 slice reduced-fat Swiss cheese

1. Preheat oven to 400°F.

2. Cut a 20" piece of parchment.

3. Line a baking sheet with aluminum foil.

4. Spread mustard on one slice of bread and ketchup on the other.

5. Add horseradish sauce to the ketchup side.

6. Place beef on one slice.

7. Add cabbage or sauerkraut and top with Swiss cheese.

8. Place the second slice of bread on top.

9. Spray both sides of the sandwich with cooking spray.

10. Fold the parchment.

11. Bake for 20 minutes.

Calories: 285 | Fat: 7 g | Protein: 24 g | Sodium: 1216 mg | Carbohydrates: 30 g | Fiber: 4 g

Thai Beef with Broccoli Slaw and Coconut Rice

Serves 2

Thai fish sauce (found in the Asian section of your grocery store) has an assertive flavor, but it adds interesting depth to this dish. You can find bagged broccoli slaw in the produce section of your grocery store. If you don't have lime juice, lemon juice will work in a pinch.

½ pound strip steak, sliced very thin

2 teaspoons Thai fish sauce

1 tablespoon lime juice

1 teaspoon olive oil

1 tablespoon fresh basil, chopped

1 tablespoon fresh cilantro, chopped

1 tablespoon onion, chopped

1 clove garlic, chopped

2 tablespoons green chili, chopped

¼ teaspoon sugar

¼ teaspoon salt

1 cup cooked brown rice (instant or regular, cooked with coconut water instead of water, according to package instructions)

1 cup broccoli slaw

1 tablespoon tamari sauce (or soy)

1. Place everything but the rice, slaw, and tamari in a zip-top bag.
2. Marinate for at least 20 minutes, up to 4 hours.
3. Preheat oven to 400ºF.
4. Cut a 20" piece of parchment.
5. Line a baking sheet with aluminum foil.
6. Place rice on center of parchment.
7. Top with beef mixture (including all juices in the bag), slaw, and tamari.
8. Toss to combine.
9. Fold the parchment.
10. Bake for 30 minutes.
11. Open parchment and broil for 5 minutes.

Calories: 277 | Fat: 11 g | Protein: 38 g | Sodium: 1241 mg | Carbohydrates: 6.5 g | Fiber: 0.5 g

Veal Cutlet with Mushroom, Spinach, and Angel Hair Pasta

Serves 1

Enjoy the tenderness of veal and the delicate texture of angel hair pasta in a creamy light sauce. This is a rich and delicious dish that you can kick up in spiciness by adding ample red pepper flakes!

3 ounces fresh refrigerated angel hair pasta

1 clove garlic, chopped

½ teaspoon olive oil

1 veal cutlet, ¼" thick

Salt and pepper to taste

5 Baby Bella or white button mushrooms, thinly sliced

⅛ teaspoon onion powder

½ cup fresh baby spinach

2 tablespoons heavy cream

2 tablespoons reduced-sodium beef broth

1 teaspoon cornstarch

1 tablespoon fresh parsley, chopped

Red pepper flakes to taste

1. Preheat oven to 400°F.
2. Cut a 20" piece of parchment.
3. Line a baking sheet with aluminum foil.
4. Soak the pasta in a bowl of hot water for 5 minutes.
5. Drain the pasta and place it on the parchment.
6. Top the pasta with garlic and olive oil.
7. Place the veal cutlet on top and season with salt and pepper.
8. Place the mushrooms on top.
9. Sprinkle the onion powder on top, followed by the spinach.
10. In a small bowl, mix cream, beef broth, and cornstarch and drizzle over the pasta, meat, and vegetables. Top with parsley.
11. Fold the parchment.
12. Bake for 15 minutes.
13. Open the packet and gently toss ingredients together, so the vegetables combine with pasta.
14. Sprinkle on dried red pepper flakes to taste.

Calories: 559 | Fat: 29 g | Protein: 38 g | Sodium: 207 mg | Carbohydrates: 38 g | Fiber: 3 g

Beef on Weck Roll-Up

Serves 1

Another specialty from my area, beef on weck sandwiches are traditionally made with roast beef slices that are cooked au jus, then piled on a roll called kimmelweck *(a hard roll topped with coarse salt and caraway seeds). Most people add ketchup and horseradish to the sandwich. Here I've re-created a lighter rendition wrapped in a tortilla.*

1 whole wheat tortilla

1 tablespoon ketchup

½ tablespoon prepared horseradish

3 slices deli roast beef

¼ teaspoon caraway seeds, plus a pinch

¼ teaspoon coarse sea salt, plus a pinch

1. Preheat oven to 400°F.
2. Cut a 20" piece of parchment.
3. Line a baking sheet with aluminum foil.
4. Place the tortilla on the parchment and spread ketchup and horseradish to within 1" of the sides.
5. Place the roast beef on top and sprinkle with ¼ teaspoon caraway and ¼ teaspoon salt.
6. Roll up the tortilla and place on the parchment seam-side down.
7. Spray the top of the tortilla with cooking spray and sprinkle the pinches of caraway and salt on top.
8. Fold the parchment.
9. Bake for 15 minutes.

Calories: 381 | Fat: 24 g | Protein: 16 g | Sodium: 2030 mg | Carbohydrates: 24 g | Fiber: 3 g

Rolled Steak

Serves 1

Steak, cheese, and mushrooms in a red sauce—that's hard to beat. Fun to make and fun to eat! Enjoy this dish with a side of green beans and some pasta with additional red sauce.

1 top round cutlet, ¼"–½" thick (about 4 ounces)

Salt and pepper to taste

1 slice provolone cheese

1 tablespoon bread crumbs

¼ teaspoon onion powder

8 fresh basil leaves

½ portobello mushroom, sliced thinly

¾ cup prepared spaghetti sauce

1. Preheat oven to 400°F.
2. Cut a 20" piece of parchment.
3. Line a baking sheet with aluminum foil.
4. Place the top round cutlet on the parchment.
5. Season with salt and pepper.
6. Cut the cheese in half and lay on top of the meat.
7. Sprinkle with bread crumbs and onion powder.
8. Layer the basil leaves across the top.
9. Spread mushrooms across the top.
10. Roll up the beef and place seam-side down on the parchment.
11. Top with spaghetti sauce.
12. Fold the parchment.
13. Bake for 30 minutes.

Calories: 583 | Fat: 30 g | Protein: 41 g | Sodium: 417 mg | Carbohydrates: 38 g | Fiber: 5 g

Steak in the Grass with Pomegranate Sauce

Serves 2

Dandelion greens are bitter, so if you enjoy bitter flavors, this dish is for you. The pomegranate sauce is thick and colorful, adding a large dose of liveliness to this dish.

1 tablespoon olive oil

1 clove garlic, chopped

2 top round cutlets, ¼"-½" thick

1 bunch dandelion greens, stems removed, about 2 mounding cups

Salt and pepper to taste

1 cup pomegranate juice (I use Pom Wonderful)

¼ teaspoon rosemary

Herb and Garlic Bread (see Chapter 7)

1. Preheat oven to 400°F.

2. Cut a 20" piece of parchment.

3. Line a baking sheet with aluminum foil.

4. Place the olive oil and garlic in a bowl and add beef.

5. Allow this to marinate about 20 minutes in the refrigerator.

6. Place the dandelions on the parchment.

7. Add the beef.

8. Drizzle with olive oil and garlic marinade.

9. Season with salt and pepper.

10. Toss to combine.

11. Fold the parchment.

12. Bake for 20 minutes.

13. While that is baking, mix juice and rosemary in 2-cup glass measuring cup. Microwave on high for about 12 minutes, or until sauce is reduced to ¼ cup.

14. Toss meat and greens. Place on Herb and Garlic Bread and drizzle with a small amount of pomegranate sauce.

If you are lucky enough to make this recipe in the spring and have access to a yard or field that hasn't been sprayed with herbicides and pesticides, go outside and pick your own dandelions. You want very young greens, those without seed heads, flowers, or buds. Wash them well and cut off the roots.

Calories: 328 | Fat: 20 g | Protein: 29 g | Sodium: 101 mg | Carbohydrates: 6 g | Fiber: 2.5 g

Beef and Pimiento Cheese Quesadillas

Serves 2

Quesadillas as a concept are so versatile—they're essentially just grilled cheese sandwiches made on tortillas. You can use prepared pimiento cheese or make your own, as directed here. This is a wonderful special treat that is an alternative to a cheeseburger.

Pimiento Cheese

¼ cup soft cream cheese from a tub

¼ cup light mayonnaise

½ cup light Velveeta cheese

½ cup shredded sharp Cheddar cheese

¼ teaspoon onion powder

¼ cup shredded Monterey jack cheese

⅛ teaspoon dry or powdered mustard

2 tablespoons pimientos, chopped

Quesadillas

2 whole wheat tortillas

¼ pound ground beef

Salt and pepper to taste

½ cup pimiento cheese

2 tablespoons ketchup (optional)

2 tablespoons mustard (optional)

2 tablespoons relish (optional)

1 thin slice of onion, broken into pieces (optional)

Pimiento Cheese

1. Place all ingredients except pimientos in a glass bowl and microwave on high for 30 seconds, then stir to combine.

2. Add pimientos. Stir to combine.

Quesadillas

1. Preheat oven to 400°F.

2. Cut a 20" piece of parchment.

3. Line a baking sheet with aluminum foil.

4. Spray the bottom of one tortilla and place on the parchment. Place ground beef on top and spread, pressing until it is evenly distributed over the tortilla, covering most of it. Season with salt and pepper.

5. Place as much pimiento cheese on top as you like and spread, covering the beef. Place any toppings you choose on the other tortilla, and then place that on top of the meat and cheese.

6. Spray the top of the tortilla.

7. Fold the parchment.

8. Bake for 20 minutes. Open packet and cut into quarters with a pizza cutter.

Calories: 852 | Fat: 57 g | Protein: 54 g | Sodium: 1581 mg | Carbohydrates: 29 g | Fiber: 3 g

Stuffed Cabbage

Serves 2

I use savoy cabbage in this recipe, because it has thinner leaves that cook more quickly than other varieties of cabbage. You can vary the filling you use in this, substituting ground turkey for the ground beef, or couscous or quinoa for the rice.

½ pound ground beef

1 cup cooked brown rice

¼ cup shredded part-skim mozzarella cheese

½ teaspoon onion powder

½ teaspoon garlic powder

Salt and pepper to taste

1 teaspoon sugar

1 15-ounce can tomato sauce

8 leaves savoy cabbage

1. Preheat oven to 400°F.

2. Cut two 20" pieces of parchment.

3. Line a baking sheet with aluminum foil.

4. Mix beef, rice, cheese, seasonings, and ½ cup tomato sauce in a bowl.

5. Cut each cabbage leaf in half, removing the thick center vein.

6. Spread ¼ cup of tomato sauce in the center of each piece of parchment.

7. Take one half leaf of cabbage and place 1 tablespoon of beef and rice filling in the center.

8. Fold in the sides, then fold up the top and bottom.

9. Place seam-side down on the parchment.

10. Repeat until you have 8 packets on each piece of parchment.

11. Pour 1 cup of tomato sauce over the contents of each packet, making sure it doesn't run off the sides of the parchment.

12. Fold parchment.

13. Bake for 50 minutes.

Calories: 604 | Fat: 15 g | Protein: 34 g | Sodium: 158 mg | Carbohydrates: 24 g | Fiber: 3 g

Lasagna Roll-Ups

Serves 1

Enjoy all the flavors of lasagna with these fun roll-ups sans a sticky pan to scrub—what could be better? If you have kids who don't like spinach, or you're just looking for a slightly crunchier texture, you can substitute broccoli.

1 sheet refrigerated fresh lasagna

⅛ pound ground beef

1 tablespoon frozen chopped spinach (defrosted and squeezed dry)

⅛ teaspoon onion powder

⅛ teaspoon garlic powder

½ teaspoon Italian seasoning

Salt and pepper to taste

⅛ cup shredded part-skim mozzarella plus 1 tablespoon (reserved)

¼ cup part-skim ricotta cheese

½ cup tomato sauce

1 tablespoon cream

1. Preheat oven to 400°F.

2. Cut a 20" piece of parchment.

3. Line a baking sheet with aluminum foil.

4. Lay the lasagna sheet on the parchment.

5. Spread the ground beef over it, pressing to flatten, and covering most of the sheet.

6. Place the spinach on top.

7. Sprinkle with onion powder, garlic powder, Italian seasoning, salt, and pepper. Sprinkle with ⅛ cup mozzarella, and then top with the ricotta, smoothing it gently.

8. Roll up the sheet and place seam-side down on the parchment.

9. Top with tomato sauce, cream, and reserved 1 tablespoon mozzarella.

10. Bake for 25 minutes.

Refrigerated, fresh pastas are now easy to find in most grocery stores. They are preferable to dried pasta because they are soft and tender and cook well in parchment.

Calories: 429 | Fat: 19 g | Protein: 38 g | Sodium: 241 mg | Carbohydrates: 25 g | Fiber: 1 g

Root Beer Beef and Broccoli

Serves 3 or 4

Have you ever cooked with root beer before? Its dark sweetness is the perfect accompaniment to beef and makes a unique and rich sauce. The broccoli serves as a colorful—and healthful—counterpoint.

¾ pound sirloin steak, sliced very thin

Salt and pepper to taste

1 clove garlic, chopped

1 teaspoon balsamic vinegar

½ cup root beer or diet root beer

2 tablespoons Worcestershire sauce

1 cup couscous, uncooked

1 cup broccoli florets

1 tablespoon cornstarch

1. Place beef, salt, pepper, garlic, balsamic vinegar, root beer, and Worcestershire sauce in a zip-top bag and marinate, refrigerated, for 2–4 hours.

2. Preheat oven to 400°F.

3. Cut a 30" piece of parchment.

4. Line a baking sheet with aluminum foil.

5. Place couscous in a bowl with 1 cup hot water and allow to stand 2–3 minutes until water is absorbed.

6. Place couscous on parchment.

7. Remove beef from bag, reserving the marinade. Place the beef on the couscous, followed by the broccoli.

8. Toss beef, broccoli, and coucous together.

9. Mix 2 tablespoons of the marinade with the cornstarch, then pour over the ingredients.

10. Fold parchment.

11. Bake for 25 minutes.

Calories: 320 | Fat: 6 g | Protein: 31 g | Sodium: 152 mg | Carbohydrates: 32 g | Fiber: 2 g

Stuffed Veal

Serves 1

Green olives add a briny flavor to this dish, which is smothered in a decadent sauce. Rolling the veal cutlets helps keep the flavors inside the meat and makes cute packets.

1 veal cutlet, ¼" thick

1 tablespoon sliced green olives

⅛ cup shredded part-skim mozzarella

1 teaspoon bread crumbs

Salt and pepper to taste

1 teaspoon Dijon mustard

1 small clove garlic

1 teaspoon olive oil

1 tablespoon white wine

1 teaspoon tomato paste

½ teaspoon Italian herb mix

1. Preheat oven to 400°F.
2. Cut a 20" piece of parchment.
3. Line a baking sheet with aluminum foil.
4. Lay the veal cutlet on the parchment.
5. Sprinkle the olives, cheese, and bread crumbs over it and season with salt and pepper.
6. Roll the cutlet up and place it seam-side down on the parchment.
7. If any stuffing falls out, just stick it back in the sides.
8. In a small bowl mix the Dijon, garlic, olive oil, wine, tomato paste, and Italian herbs, then pour over the veal.
9. Fold the parchment.
10. Bake for 20 minutes.

Calories: 270 | Fat: 18 g | Protein: 23 g | Sodium: 229 mg | Carbohydrates: 4 g | Fiber: 1 g

Baked Fontina with Salami

Serves 6

This dish is a wonderful spread or dip that everyone can share. It's perfect as an appetizer or as an accompaniment to a soup such as Italian wedding or minestrone. You might also want to enjoy it as a special lunch, paired with a bowl of ripe cherries.

½ pound fontina cheese

1 ounce light or reduced-fat salami, diced

¼ cup roasted red pepper, diced

¼ cup fresh basil, chopped

Salt and pepper to taste

½ cup arugula, roughly chopped

Crackers or bread (whole wheat or whole grain)

1. Preheat oven to 400°F.
2. Cut a 20" piece of parchment.
3. Line a baking sheet with aluminum foil.
4. Place the cheese on the parchment.
5. Top with salami, peppers, and basil.
6. Season with salt and pepper.
7. Fold the parchment.
8. Bake for 15 minutes.
9. Open parchment and gently mix to distribute ingredients.
10. Top with arugula.
11. Serve with whole wheat crackers or bread.

Substitute your favorite Italian deli meat for the salami, such as mortadella, prosciutto, capicola, or sopressato. If you'd like to go vegetarian, switch out the meat for some frozen spinach that's been squeezed dry, or try some sliced portobello mushrooms.

Calories: 173 | Fat: 13 g | Protein: 11 g | Sodium: 377 mg | Carbohydrates: 3.5 g | Fiber: 0.5 g

Indian Beef Wraps

Serves 2 or 3

Tired of hamburgers? This is a great recipe for kids who can tolerate spice or anyone willing to try familiar ingredients with new flavors added for different tastes. The list of ingredients looks long, but this comes together in no time.

½ pound ground beef

½ cup frozen peas

1 tablespoon chopped green chiles

½ teaspoon garlic powder

½ teaspoon onion powder

1 teaspoon lemon juice

¼ cup cilantro, chopped

2 tablespoons bottled chili sauce (the type sold next to the ketchup in glass bottles), plus a little extra for topping

Pinch of ground cloves

⅛ teaspoon cumin

⅛ teaspoon coriander

⅛ teaspoon cardamom

⅛ teaspoon cinnamon

1 tablespoon plain low-fat or nonfat yogurt

Salt and pepper to taste

3 whole wheat tortillas

1. Preheat oven to 400°F.
2. Cut a 20" piece of parchment.
3. Line a baking sheet with aluminum foil.
4. Mix all ingredients except tortillas in a medium bowl.
5. Place ⅓ of mixture on each tortilla.
6. Roll up the tortillas and lay them seam-side down on the parchment.
7. Top each with a thin line of chili sauce.
8. Fold parchment paper.
9. Bake for 25 minutes.

Calories: 309 | Fat: 11 g | Protein: 26 g | Sodium: 253 mg | Carbohydrates: 24 g | Fiber: 2.5 g

Roast Beef Hash Brown

Serves 2

They think of everything these days! Look for refrigerated cooked potatoes to make this meal even easier to assemble. If you don't like horseradish Cheddar cheese (or can't find it), substitute another with a strong flavor, such as extra sharp Cheddar.

1¼ cup refrigerated shredded cooked potatoes

1 tablespoon olive oil

Salt and pepper to taste

3 slices deli roast beef (organic if possible)

2 slices horseradish Cheddar cheese

¼ teaspoon Italian seasoning

1. Preheat the oven to 400°F.

2. Cut a 20" piece of parchment.

3. Line a baking sheet with aluminum foil.

4. Spray a 6" × 6" circle on the parchment with cooking spray.

5. Place potatoes on it and press to form 6" × 6" circle.

6. Drizzle olive oil over the top and season with salt and pepper.

7. Bake uncovered for 25 minutes.

8. Broil for 2 minutes. Remove from oven and place the roast beef on top.

9. Rip the cheese into smaller pieces and place on top of the beef.

10. Sprinkle with the Italian seasoning.

11. Return to the oven at 400°F and bake about 5 minutes until the cheese melts.

> Refrigerated cooked potatoes can be found in the dairy or produce section of your store. If you can't find them, use frozen cooked shredded potatoes that have been defrosted.

Calories: 330 | Fat: 19 g | Protein: 16 g | Sodium: 227 mg | Carbohydrates: 26 g | Fiber: 1.5 g

Sloppy Joe Pitas

Serves 3

Plan to eat this one with a knife and fork. Here you get all the great flavors of a Sloppy Joe with almost no cleanup. You could also make this in rolled-up tortillas for a Southwest twist. Serve with a dollop of yogurt or sour cream for a creamy addition.

¼ red bell pepper, chopped

¼ large onion, chopped

½ tablespoon olive oil

½ pound lean ground beef

2 tablespoons tomato sauce

1 tablespoon Worcestershire sauce

4 tablespoons bottled chili sauce, with extra for topping

3 whole wheat pitas

1. Preheat the oven to 400°F.

2. Cut three 20" pieces of parchment.

3. Line a baking sheet with aluminum foil.

4. Place the pepper, onion, and oil in a glass measuring cup or bowl and microwave on High for 3 minutes.

5. Mix vegetables with beef and add tomato sauce, Worcestershire, and chili sauce.

6. Cut ⅛ to ¼ off the end of each pita and gently open the pita along the exposed side.

7. Stuff ⅓ of the meat mixture into each pita.

8. Spray each side of the pitas with cooking spray and place each one on a separate piece of parchment.

9. Fold the parchment.

10. Bake for 20 minutes. Serve with additional chili sauce.

Calories: 366 | Fat: 13 g | Protein: 28 g | Sodium: 399 mg | Carbohydrates: 35 g | Fiber: 4.5 g

CHAPTER 5

Seafood Dishes

The original *en papillote* recipes feature seafood, because fish is perfectly suited to parchment paper cooking. The parchment steams the fish and seals all the flavors in, resulting in deliciously moist dishes—every single time. I've used a variety of seafood in these recipes. You can substitute nearly any fish you like or have available in any dish and it'll still be delectable.

Sole with Crabmeat

Serves 4

When I was first married, I experimented a lot to practice my cooking skills. I found a recipe called Sole en Papillote, which involved wrapping sole and crabmeat in wax paper. I've never forgotten how delicious it was and have re-created it here with parchment paper.

8 ounces crab (pasteurized is fine, but don't use imitation crab)

6 ounces (one jar) crème fraiche or light sour cream

1 teaspoon dried dill

2 tablespoons melted butter

2 tablespoons white wine

4 teaspoons lemon juice

Salt and pepper to taste

4 sole fillets

Zest of 1 lemon

Fresh parsley

1. Preheat oven to 400°F.

2. Cut two pieces of 20" parchment, or four 12" pieces. (You can create this dish as two packets with two servings each, or as four individual packets.)

3. Line a baking sheet with aluminum foil.

4. In a small bowl, mix crab, crème fraiche or sour cream, dill, butter, white wine, lemon juice, salt, and pepper.

5. In each packet, place the sole on the bottom, then cover with crab mixture.

6. Sprinkle lemon zest on top and place two sprigs of parsley on each piece.

7. Fold the parchment.

8. Bake for 20 minutes.

Crème fraiche is a traditional French dairy product that is similar to sour cream, but thicker. You may be able to find it in the gourmet cheese or dairy section of your supermarket. If not, sour cream works fine as a replacement.

Calories: 277 | Fat: 14 g | Protein: 34 g | Sodium: 312 mg | Carbohydrates: 3 g | Fiber: 0 g

Greek Shrimp

Serves 4

My family always asks me to make this! The shrimp cooks in the tomato juices and comes out sweet and tender. You could make this with rice on the bottom of the packets if you like (about ½ cup of rice per packet), or serve it on the side. Another option is to add sliced black olives for some regional flair.

2 scallions

1 14-ounce can stewed tomatoes, drained

1 pound raw shrimp (peeled and deveined, with tails removed)

1 teaspoon Greek seasoning (use oregano as a substitute)

Salt and pepper to taste

½ cup fat-free feta cheese

1. Preheat oven to 375ºF.
2. Cut a 24" piece of parchment.
3. Line a baking sheet with aluminum foil.
4. Slice the scallions into thin rounds.
5. Chop the drained tomatoes into 1" pieces.
6. Place the shrimp in the center of the parchment.
7. Top with the tomatoes, then the scallions.
8. Sprinkle with Greek seasoning, salt, and pepper.
9. Crumble the feta cheese over the top.
10. Fold the parchment.
11. Bake for 20 minutes.

Calories: 174 | Fat: 5.5 g | Protein: 24 g | Sodium: 533 mg | Carbohydrates: 7.5 g | Fiber: 1 g

Tilapia with Smoked Salmon

Serves 1

I'm a sucker for lox and bagels, so I came up with this low-cal alternative, which is hearty enough for dinner and sure to be a hit. (It was a hit on my blog!)

1 tilapia fillet

1 tablespoon light cream cheese

⅛ teaspoon dried dill (if you have fresh, use that)

Salt and pepper to taste

1–2 ounces smoked salmon

½ teaspoon fresh lemon juice

½ whole wheat bagel

Garlic oil or butter

1. Preheat oven to 400°F.
2. Cut a 20" piece of parchment.
3. Line a baking sheet with aluminum foil.
4. Place tilapia on parchment.
5. Spread the cream cheese over it.
6. Sprinkle half of the dill on top.
7. Season with salt and pepper.
8. Place the salmon on top.
9. Drizzle the lemon juice on top.
10. Sprinkle remaining dill on top.
11. Fold the parchment.
12. Bake for 20 minutes.
13. While the dish is baking, slice the bagels in half into 2 slices.
14. Toast the bagel slices and brush with garlic oil or butter. Serve with the fish.

Tilapia is my go-to fish. It's mild and goes with just about anything you can think of. If you buy it fresh and farmed in the United States, it's also sustainable (frozen tilapia generally comes from Taiwan or China, where it is not raised sustainably). It's also affordable, making it perfect for families on a budget.

Calories: 277 | Fat: 7.3 g | Protein: 38 g | Sodium: 677 mg | Carbohydrates: 16 g | Fiber: 2 g

Green Tea Salmon with Ginger

Serves 1

Salmon is a wonderful, firm, filling fish. Cooking it in tea gives it a delicate aroma and scent, complemented by the honey and lemon juice. I like to leave the tea bag in the parchment packet so everyone knows how the food was cooked, but be sure to tell those you are serving not to eat it!

1 salmon fillet (¾ pound)

Salt and pepper to taste

¼ cup water

1 green tea bag (string and tags cut off)

1" piece of fresh ginger, peeled

¼ cup baby spinach leaves

6" green part of a green onion, cut into 4 sections

¼ cup cooked shucked edamame

1 teaspoon honey

1 tablespoon lemon juice

1. Preheat oven to 400°F.

2. Cut a 20" piece of parchment and place it on top of a piece of aluminum foil cut to the same size.

3. Line a baking sheet with aluminum foil.

4. Place the salmon on the parchment and season with salt and pepper.

5. Pour ¼ cup water into a glass measuring cup. Add the tea bag and ginger to the cup and bring the water to a boil in the microwave. Allow to steep about 5 minutes.

6. Place the spinach, green onion, and edamame on top of the salmon.

7. Stir honey and lemon juice into the tea.

8. Pour the tea over the salmon and vegetables, nestling the tea bag and ginger into the vegetables.

9. Fold the parchment.

10. Bake for 20 minutes.

> Edamame, or soy beans, can be found packaged in your produce department, or you can buy them frozen and boil them yourself. They are also now available shucked and frozen.

Calories: 330 | Fat: 13 g | Protein: 35 g | Sodium: 317 mg | Carbohydrates: 23 g | Fiber: 5 g

Shrimp with Bok Choy

Serves 2

This dish is simply glorious—bright and colorful and packed with flavor even though it has just four ingredients. I love cooking noodles in parchment! Simple and tasty, with no cleanup—what else could you want?

16 ounces (31–35 count) frozen shrimp, peeled and deveined

1 small clove garlic, chopped, or ⅛ teaspoon garlic powder

1 head baby bok choy, cleaned and roughly chopped

2 tablespoons hoisin sauce

1. Preheat oven to 400ºF.

2. Cut a 20" piece of parchment.

3. Line a baking sheet with aluminum foil.

4. Place all the ingredients on the parchment and lightly toss them together with a fork.

5. Fold the parchment.

6. Bake for 12–15 minutes (the larger and flatter you make the packet, the faster this will cook).

Calories: 117 | Fat: 2 g | Protein: 15 g | Sodium: 372 mg | Carbohydrates: 9 g | Fiber: 2 g

BBQ Salmon

Serves 2

I recently read a great cookbook called Cooking in the South, *by Johnnie Gabriel, who is Paula Deen's cousin. One recipe features a salmon dish with a BBQ-like sauce. That recipe inspired me to make my own version for parchment paper cooking.*

1 pound salmon (use as one piece, or cut in half to create two separate packets)

2 tablespoons melted butter

2 tablespoons tamari or soy sauce

1 tablespoon yellow mustard

1 tablespoon Worcestershire sauce

⅛ teaspoon onion powder

⅛ teaspoon garlic powder

4 tablespoons condensed tomato soup

1½ teaspoons apple cider vinegar

2 tablespoons brown sugar

Salt and pepper to taste

1. Preheat oven to 400°F.
2. Cut a 20" piece of parchment.
3. Line a baking sheet with aluminum foil.
4. Place the salmon on the parchment paper.
5. Place all the other ingredients in a glass bowl or measuring cup and microwave on High for 2 minutes. Stir it well.
6. Pour half of the mixture over the salmon (reserving half).
7. Fold up the parchment.
8. Bake for 25 minutes.
9. Serve with the reserved BBQ sauce on the side.

Calories: 483 | Fat: 23 g | Protein: 54 g | Sodium: 1531 mg | Carbohydrates: 16 g | Fiber: 2.5 g

Halibut with Rye Dip

Serves 1

Simple to put together, this dish also looks appetizing when cooked. It's an ideal dish to make after a party when you have leftover dip and want to try to get back on the straight and narrow with your diet by eating fish.

1 halibut fillet (about ⅓ pound)

¼ cup rye dip

Salt and pepper to taste

10–12 asparagus stalks, trimmed

1 lemon wedge

1. Preheat oven to 400°F.
2. Cut a 20" piece of parchment.
3. Line a baking sheet with aluminum foil.
4. Place the halibut fillet on the parchment.
5. Spread the dip over it, then sprinkle with salt and pepper.
6. Lay the asparagus stalks on top and squeeze the lemon over it.
7. Fold the parchment.
8. Bake for 20 minutes.

You can find rye dip at your grocery store or deli. This is the sour cream–based dip that is commonly put in a hollowed-out round loaf of rye bread. Here's another use for that delicious dip so you can enjoy it in a healthier way by using a tiny bit and pairing it with more nutritious ingredients.

Calories: 220 | Fat: 3.5 g | Protein: 29 g | Sodium: 64 mg | Carbohydrates: 20 g | Fiber: 5.5 g

Mussels with Butter, Wine, and Garlic

Serves 2

I spent childhood summer vacations in Maine, where we found our own mussels on the beach and ate them the same day for lunch or dinner. Make like you're on the seashore and serve with a loaf of multigrain bread to sop up the juices. (If you're a crafty type, save the beautiful blue shells for a special project!)

50 mussels

3 tablespoons butter

2 cloves garlic, chopped

3 tablespoons white wine

Salt and pepper to taste

2 tablespoons fresh parsley, chopped

1. Preheat oven to 400°F.
2. Cut a 20" piece of parchment.
3. Line a baking sheet with aluminum foil.
4. Clean and scrub the mussels, pulling off any beards.
5. Discard any mussels that are open.
6. Place mussels on the parchment.
7. Place the butter and garlic in a small glass bowl and microwave until the butter is melted and begins to bubble.
8. Stir in the white wine, salt, and pepper.
9. Pour the mixture over the mussels.
10. Sprinkle parsley over the mussels.
11. Fold the parchment.
12. Bake for 15 minutes.
13. Discard any mussels that did not open while cooking.
14. Be sure to dip the mussels in the sauce at the bottom of the packet when enjoying.

Calories: 361 | Fat: 22 g | Protein: 28 g | Sodium: 818 mg | Carbohydrates: 12 g | Fiber: 0 g

Chard-Wrapped Haddock

Serves 2

This was inspired by Hawaiian cooking, in which fish and other foods are wrapped in ti leaves. The result is an incredibly moist dish with all the flavors locked in. Enjoy this little bit of a luau!

2–3 Swiss chard leaves, stems removed

½ pound haddock fillet

Salt and pepper to taste

2 mushrooms, thinly sliced

1 tablespoon melted butter

1 tablespoon teriyaki sauce

1 tablespoon fresh lemon juice

Green end of 1 scallion, chopped

1. Preheat oven to 400ºF.
2. Cut a 20" piece of parchment.
3. Line a baking sheet with aluminum foil.
4. Lay the chard leaves on the parchment.
5. Place the haddock so it is lying across all of the leaves, along an edge.
6. Season the fish with salt and pepper.
7. Place the mushrooms on top of the fish.
8. Drizzle melted butter, teriyaki sauce, and lemon juice over fish.
9. Scatter the scallion on top.
10. Fold over the chard leaves and tuck under the fish.
11. Fold the parchment.
12. Bake for 15 minutes.

Ti leaves are used in traditional Hawaiian cuisine as a cooking container. Fish, pork, or vegetables are wrapped in the leaves and cooked over hot stones. The leaves seal in the moisture, just as parchment paper does.

Calories: 144 | Fat: 6.5 g | Protein: 18 g | Sodium: 561 mg | Carbohydrates: 3.5 g | Fiber: 1 g

"Paper Bag" Tilapia

Serves 1

The Bubble Room is a wonderful restaurant on Captiva Island in South Florida that serves a signature dish called the Eddie Fisherman. They coat the grouper in an amazing mixture of pecans and brown sugar and cook it in a brown paper bag. The bag is cut open in front of you, steaming. This dish replicates the flavors, but with a more sustainable, budget-friendly fish.

1 tilapia fillet

1 tablespoon butter

2½ tablespoons pecans, chopped

1 tablespoon brown sugar

1 tablespoon orange juice

1 tablespoon lemon juice

1 teaspoon cornstarch

Salt and pepper to taste

1. Preheat oven to 400°F.

2. Cut a 20" piece of parchment.

3. Line a baking sheet with aluminum foil.

4. Place tilapia on parchment.

5. In a small glass bowl, bowl, melt the butter, then stir in the other ingredients.

6. Drizzle over fish.

7. Fold the parchment.

8. Bake for 10 minutes.

Calories: 427 | Fat: 27 g | Protein: 31 g | Sodium: 186 mg | Carbohydrates: 18 g | Fiber: 2 g

Halibut with Spinach Sauce

Serves 4

Inspired by a cookbook called Fishes and Dishes *that I bought on a trip to Alaska, this recipe results in halibut that remains beautifully moist. The spinach gives it a bright color as well. You'll want to clean your packet of the very last drop!*

4 halibut fillets (¼ pound apiece)

3 teaspoons Dijon mustard

½ cup light sour cream

½ cup plain low-fat or nonfat yogurt

¼ teaspoon dried minced onion

¼ teaspoon dried dill

4 ounces frozen chopped spinach, squeezed dry

Salt and pepper to taste

Lemon wedges

1. Preheat oven to 400°F.
2. Cut four 20" pieces of parchment.
3. Line a baking sheet with aluminum foil.
4. Place one fillet on each piece of parchment.
5. In a bowl, mix all the other ingredients except the lemon wedges.
6. Spoon ¼ of the sauce on top of each fillet.
7. Fold the parchment.
8. Bake for 17 minutes.
9. Serve with wedges of lemon to squeeze over the dish.

Calories: 165 | Fat: 6.5 g | Protein: 20 g | Sodium: 109 mg | Carbohydrates: 6 g | Fiber: 1 g

Linguine with Clam Sauce

Serves 1

Some people think clams are difficult to cook. Not so! This no-fuss method produces a flavorful pasta with clams that debunks the myth.

4½ ounces fresh, refrigerated angel hair pasta

1 tablespoon fresh parsley, chopped

1 large clove of garlic, chopped

1 tablespoon melted butter

1½ tablespoons olive oil

2 tablespoons white wine

1½ tablespoons lemon juice

1 cup chopped clams, with juice (canned, or frozen clams that have been defrosted, with juice)

1 teaspoon cornstarch

Salt and pepper to taste

¼ teaspoon dried oregano

Pinch of red pepper flakes

1. Preheat oven to 400°F.

2. Cut a 20" piece of parchment.

3. Line a baking sheet with aluminum foil.

4. Soak the pasta in 3 cups hot water in a glass measuring cup, bowl, or in the sink for about 5 minutes.

5. Remove the pasta and place on the parchment.

6. Top with parsley and chopped garlic.

7. In a small bowl, mix butter, oil, wine, lemon juice, and juice from clams with cornstarch. Pour over pasta.

8. Add clams, salt, pepper, oregano, and pepper flakes.

9. Gently toss the mixture.

10. Fold the parchment.

11. Bake for 15 minutes.

Calories: 675 | Fat: 35 g | Protein: 38 g | Sodium: 253 mg | Carbohydrates: 52 g | Fiber: 2 g

Salmon with Mustard Sauce

Serves 4

I dare you to find a simpler way to make salmon that produces this much flavor. The lemon juice, mustard, and brown sugar combine to make a tangy dark brown sauce that perfectly complements the richness in the fish. You can use salmon steaks, but I find fillets are easier to work with and have fewer bones.

2 tablespoons lemon juice

2 tablespoons Dijon mustard

2 tablespoons brown sugar

4 individual salmon fillets (¼–⅓ pound apiece) or 1 large fillet (1–1¼ pounds)

Salt and pepper to taste

1. Preheat oven to 400°F.

2. Cut a 30" piece of parchment.

3. Line a baking sheet with aluminum foil.

4. Mix the lemon juice, mustard, and brown sugar in a small bowl.

5. Place the salmon in the center of the parchment paper.

6. Spoon sauce over salmon.

7. Sprinkle with salt and pepper.

8. Fold the parchment.

9. If you're making one family-size fillet, bake for 30 minutes. If you're making four individual pieces, place each fillet on a 20" piece of parchment, and bake for only 15 minutes.

Calories: 226 | Fat: 7 g | Protein: 33 g | Sodium: 376 mg | Carbohydrates: 7 g | Fiber: 1.5 g

Mahi-Mahi with Fennel and Blood Orange

Serves 1

Blood oranges have a wow factor when you cut them open and find a gorgeous deep red surprise. The orange and delicate fennel flavor make an elegant topping for this firm white fish. Cod, haddock, sea bass, or halibut can be used in place of the mahi-mahi.

1 mahi-mahi fillet (about ⅓ pound)

¼ fennel bulb very thinly sliced, plus ⅛ cup chopped greens from the top (reserved)

½ tablespoon olive oil

Salt and pepper to taste

Juice of half of 1 blood orange

1 slice of blood orange

2 tablespoons fresh cilantro, chopped

1. Preheat oven to 400°F.
2. Cut a 20" piece of parchment.
3. Line a baking sheet with aluminum foil.
4. Place the fish on the parchment and top with the fennel bulb slices.
5. Drizzle the olive oil on top and season with salt and pepper.
6. Pour the juice on top.
7. Add the orange slice, the cilantro, and the chopped greens from the fennel.
8. Fold the parchment.
9. Bake for 24 minutes.

Blood oranges are oranges with a crimson-colored center. They are sweet like regular oranges, but have a bit of a tang to them. If you can't find a blood orange, you can substitute a regular orange.

Calories: 221 | Fat: 9 g | Protein: 25 g | Sodium: 975 mg | Carbohydrates: 9 g | Fiber: 4.7 g

Scallops Gratin

Serves 4

Soft, tender scallops in a lovely lemon-butter sauce topped with crunchy bread crumbs make this dish something you'll return to again and again. Make sure you rinse the scallops well to remove any grit and peel off the little muscle on the side of the scallops before cooking.

1½ pounds sea scallops

2 tablespoons butter

2 tablespoons lemon juice

1 teaspoon marjoram

¼ teaspoon lemon zest

Salt and pepper to taste

4 tablespoons bread crumbs

Lemon wedges

1. Preheat oven to 400°F.
2. Cut a 20" piece of parchment.
3. Line a baking sheet with aluminum foil.
4. Clean scallops and place them on the parchment.
5. Melt butter in a small glass bowl in the microwave.
6. Drizzle butter over scallops.
7. Drizzle lemon juice over scallops.
8. Sprinkle marjoram and lemon zest on top and season with salt and pepper.
9. Fold the parchment.
10. Bake for 25 minutes.
11. Open packet and sprinkle bread crumbs on top.
12. Spray the top of the bread crumbs with cooking spray.
13. Return to the oven with the packet open and broil for 3 minutes.
14. Serve with lemon wedges.

Calories: 268 | Fat: 8.5 g | Protein: 40 g | Sodium: 559 mg | Carbohydrates: 5 g | Fiber: 0.5 g

Bruschetta Fish

Serves 1

The flavor of this dish is reminiscent of bruschetta. If you serve it with some crispy garlic bread, you'll enjoy all of the textures and flavors of the classic Italian crowd-pleaser. Tilapia gives it ample protein to make it a complete meal.

2 tablespoons spaghetti sauce

1 tilapia fillet (about ⅓ pound) or other white fish

3 heaping tablespoons diced tomatoes and juice

⅛ teaspoon onion powder

⅛ teaspoon garlic powder

Salt and pepper to taste

1 tablespoon balsamic vinaigrette dressing (or Italian dressing)

½ teaspoon dried basil

1 tablespoon part-skim mozzarella cheese

1. Preheat oven to 400°F.

2. Cut a 20" piece of parchment.

3. Line a baking sheet with aluminum foil.

4. Spread the spaghetti sauce on the parchment in roughly the shape of the fish fillet.

5. Place fish on top.

6. Add all other ingredients, ending with mozzarella sprinkled on top.

7. Fold the parchment.

8. Bake for 15 minutes.

Calories: 312 | Fat: 11 g | Protein: 47 g | Sodium: 343 mg | Carbohydrates: 8 g | Fiber: 1.5 g

Mom's Marinated Shrimp with Rice

Serves 4

My mom has been making a version of this dish as long as I can remember. Sometimes she serves the shrimp as an entrée, but sometimes she serves it alone as an appetizer. Marinating the shrimp loads it with flavor and wakes up your taste buds, so if time allows, don't skimp!

1 pound shell-on fresh shrimp, peeled and deveined

2 tablespoons olive oil

1 tablespoon Worcestershire sauce

½ teaspoon garlic powder

½ teaspoon paprika

1 teaspoon Italian seasoning

¼ teaspoon dry/powdered mustard

1 tablespoon fresh lemon juice

1 tablespoon fresh parsley, roughly chopped

1 teaspoon pickle juice (sweet or sour—use ½ teaspoon apple cider vinegar if you don't have a jar of pickles in your fridge)

Salt and pepper to taste

1½ cups cooked black, mahogany, or brown rice (cooked until very dry)

1. Place the shrimp in a large zip-top bag and add all the other ingredients except rice.

2. Squish the bag to distribute everything. Marinate shrimp in the refrigerator for at least 20 minutes, up to 4 hours.

3. Preheat oven to 400°F.

4. Cut a 20" piece of parchment.

5. Line a baking sheet with aluminum foil.

6. Place the rice on the parchment.

7. Pour shrimp and marinade over the rice and toss, coating the rice.

8. Fold the parchment.

9. Bake for 25 minutes, until all the shrimp is pink.

If you've never eaten black (or mahogany) rice, give it a try. It has a beautiful color, a deeper flavor than brown rice, and is loaded with antioxidants. If you can't find black rice, brown rice still makes a delicious substitute.

Calories: 279 | Fat: 9 g | Protein: 18 g | Sodium: 170 mg | Carbohydrates: 10 g | Fiber: 1 g

Mahi-Mahi with Kimchi

Serves 1

Note that mahi-mahi can come in a variety of thicknesses. If you have a very thin piece, this dish may only need to cook for about 25 minutes. If the piece is thicker than 1", it will likely need at least another 10 minutes to cook completely.

1 mahi-mahi fillet (about ⅓ pound)

Salt and pepper to taste

1 chopped scallion, green and white parts

1 cup prepared kimchi

½ teaspoon sesame oil

½ tablespoon tamari (or soy sauce)

1. Preheat oven to 400°F.
2. Cut a 20" piece of parchment.
3. Line a baking sheet with aluminum foil.
4. Place the fish on the parchment and season with salt and pepper.
5. Top with scallions and kimchi.
6. Add sesame oil and tamari and toss the vegetables.
7. Fold the parchment.
8. Bake for about 30 minutes, depending on thickness.

You can buy kimchi, a Korean fermented cabbage and vegetable condiment, in the refrigerated produce section or Asian foods section of your grocery store. Kimchi can be very spicy, so you should taste it before using to determine how spicy a particular brand is. If it is super spicy, swap out half with some Asian slaw, found in the produce section of your grocery store. You can substitute traditional slaw.

Calories: 124 | Fat: 2.5 g | Protein: 15 g | Sodium: 745 mg | Carbohydrates: 9.5 g | Fiber: 5 g

Tropical Cod

Serves 2

You can try many different fish in this recipe—it is excellent with salmon, halibut, or mahi-mahi. The fruit flavors meld together to taste almost like a smoothie, which is one of my favorite treats.

2 pieces of cod (about ⅓ pound)

Salt and pepper to taste

½ cup diced fresh mango

½ cup diced fresh pineapple

½ cup diced fresh papaya

1 tablespoon melted butter

⅛ cup orange juice

2 teaspoons lime juice

2 teaspoons lemon juice

1 tablespoon cornstarch

⅛ cup coconut cream (available canned in the Mexican foods section of the grocery store)

1 teaspoon zest from lemon, lime, or orange, or a combination

1. Preheat oven to 400°F.
2. Cut a 20" piece of parchment.
3. Line a baking sheet with aluminum foil.
4. Place the fish on the parchment and season with salt and pepper.
5. Place all the fresh fruit on top.
6. In a small bowl, mix butter, orange juice, lime juice, lemon juice, and cornstarch.
7. Pour over the fish and fruit.
8. Add coconut cream and zest.
9. Fold the parchment carefully (because there will be a lot of juice).
10. Bake for 30 minutes.

Calories: 217 | Fat: 10 g | Protein: 16 g | Sodium: 125 mg | Carbohydrates: 19 g | Fiber: 2.5 g

Clam Bake in a Packet

Serves 1

Close your eyes as you open this packet and you'll be transported to the New England shore. This packet includes all you need for a complete clam bake—except the sand.

6 baby red potatoes

1 cod fillet, ¼ pound

6 littleneck clams in the shell

½ ear of fresh corn, or 1 small ear

2 tablespoons butter

1 clove garlic, chopped

⅛ teaspoon dill

1 tablespoon fresh lemon juice

Salt and pepper to taste

1. Preheat oven to 400°F.

2. Cut a 20" piece of parchment.

3. Line a baking sheet with aluminum foil.

4. Prick the potatoes all over and microwave on High for about 3 minutes, or until cooked through.

5. Halve the potatoes.

6. Place the cod on the parchment. Add the potatoes.

7. Scrub the clams, discarding any that are open. Place them on the parchment. Add the corn.

8. In a small glass bowl place butter, garlic, dill, and lemon juice. Microwave until the butter is melted. Stir to combine.

9. Pour butter mixture over the contents of the parchment packet. Season with salt and pepper.

10. Fold the parchment.

11. Bake for 25 minutes. Remove packet from the oven and allow it to rest about 3 minutes.

12. Discard any clams that did not open.

13. Enjoy the packet, making sure to dip everything in the sauce at the bottom.

Calories: 580 | Fat: 26 g | Protein: 46 g | Sodium: 407 mg | Carbohydrates: 44 g | Fiber: 5 g

Stuffed Trout

Serves 2

I've yet to meet someone who dislikes this dish—it's always a hit! The trout emerges moist and tender from the packet, with satisfying herb stuffing to enjoy. It also looks impressive, as if you spent a lot of time in the kitchen. (Don't tell them otherwise!)

2 whole rainbow trout fillets about 5–6 inches long (skin on, two sides still attached to each other)

Salt and pepper to taste

3 pieces whole wheat bread

½ teaspoon dill

2 teaspoons onion, chopped

1 tablespoon fresh parsley, chopped

2 tablespoons melted butter, plus 1 tablespoon for sauce

4 teaspoons fresh lemon juice, plus 1 tablespoon for sauce

1 tablespoon skim milk

1. Preheat oven to 400ºF.

2. Cut a 20" piece of parchment.

3. Line a baking sheet with aluminum foil.

4. Place the fillets on parchment, skin down, and season with salt and pepper.

5. In a bowl, shred the bread, then add the dill, onion, parsley, melted butter, lemon juice, milk, and more salt and pepper. Mix.

6. Place half of the mixture on one side of each piece of trout (use where the backbone would be as a divider). Fold the other half of the fish over the top, so the skin is facing up. Repeat with other piece of trout.

7. Fold the parchment.

8. Bake for 25 minutes. Remove the packet from the oven and allow it to rest about 3 minutes.

9. In the meantime, mix additional 1 tablespoon butter and 1 tablespoon lemon juice in a small bowl and microwave for 15 seconds.

10. Open the packet. To serve, open the fish up, so the skin sides are both down, and spoon the sauce over the fish and stuffing.

Calories: 358 | Fat: 17 g | Protein: 29 g | Sodium: 385 mg | Carbohydrates: 21 g | Fiber: 2 g

Tuna Steaks with Wasabi Mayonnaise

Serves 2

The wasabi mayonnaise gives the tuna a huge kick (use less wasabi if you don't like spicy foods). You can also vary this recipe by adding ½ cup of cooked brown rice to each packet before adding the fish. Up the cooking time if you prefer your tuna steaks well done; the cooking time here delivers rare steaks.

2 tuna steaks (about ⅓ pound apiece)

¼ cup light mayonnaise

1 teaspoon tamari (or soy sauce)

1 teaspoon lemon juice

¼ teaspoon grated fresh ginger

1 teaspoon wasabi paste

1. Preheat oven to 400°F.

2. Cut a 20" piece of parchment.

3. Line a baking sheet with aluminum foil.

4. Place the tuna steaks on parchment.

5. Mix the remaining ingredients together in a small bowl and spread on top of steaks.

6. Fold the parchment.

7. Bake about 10–12 minutes for rare steaks.

Wasabi is also known as Japanese horseradish. It has a distinctive bright green color and is very, very spicy.

Calories: 255 | Fat: 12 g | Protein: 30 g | Sodium: 248 mg | Carbohydrates: 5.5 g | Fiber: 0 g

Tilapia with Mustard Yogurt Sauce

Serves 2

Tilapia is the perfect foil for a creamy, tangy sauce such as this. If you don't have fresh chives, substitute finely chopped tops of green onions. If you don't have fresh chives or green onions on hand, go for dried chives (but as a last resort).

2 tilapia fillets (about ⅓ pound apiece)

Salt and pepper to taste

¼ cup plain nonfat yogurt

1 teaspoon Dijon mustard

1 tablespoon fresh chives, chopped

2 teaspoons fresh lemon juice

1 teaspoon cornstarch

1. Preheat oven to 400ºF.

2. Cut a 20" piece of parchment.

3. Line a baking sheet with aluminum foil.

4. Place the fish on parchment.

5. Season with salt and pepper.

6. In a small bowl mix remaining ingredients, then spread over the fish.

7. Fold the parchment.

8. Bake for 15 minutes.

Calories: 245 | Fat: 5.5 g | Protein: 46 g | Sodium: 119 mg | Carbohydrates: 3.5 g | Fiber: 0 g

Asparagus with Blue Cheese

Halibut with Spinach Sauce

Brussels Sprouts with Pumpkin Seed Oil and Pecans

Herb and Garlic Bread

Rustic Apple Tart

Caramel Pears

Chicken Française

Rice Pilaf

Sloppy Joe Pitas

Salmon with Cold Cilantro Yogurt Sauce

Serves 2

I love the contrast of the cool, creamy yogurt sauce with the salmon in this dish. If you have leftover yogurt sauce, save it and use it as a sauce for chicken or in a pita sandwich. Lemon Chicken with Peanut Sauce (see Chapter 2) is also good dipped in it.

2 salmon fillets (about ⅓ pound apiece)

2 sprigs fresh parsley

1 cup plain low-fat or nonfat yogurt

1 peeled and diced small cucumber

2 cups fresh cilantro, chopped

1 tablespoon fresh lime juice

Salt and pepper to taste

1. Preheat oven to 400°F.
2. Cut a 20" piece of parchment.
3. Line a baking sheet with aluminum foil.
4. Place the salmon on parchment and top with parsley.
5. Fold the parchment.
6. Bake for 20 minutes.
7. While the fish is cooking, mix the other ingredients in a small bowl.
8. To serve, top the salmon with the yogurt sauce.

Calories: 308 | Fat: 9 g | Protein: 47 g | Sodium: 674 mg | Carbohydrates: 11 g | Fiber: 2.5 g

CHAPTER 6

Vegetable Dishes

Are you tired of boiling or steaming your veggies? Try making them in parchment. These dishes produce colorful, fun results that will interest your whole family in eating their vegetables. Parchment seals in the flavors and brings what could be boring old side dishes to life.

Orange-Scented Carrots with Dill

Serves 4

The orange juice, zest, and dill in this recipe bring the carrots to life—you'll be surprised how these ingredients make the inherent flavor of the carrots pop. Use fresh dill if you have any available; otherwise, dried works fine.

½ pound baby carrots (cut in half lengthwise) or 4 whole carrots (peeled and cut into coins)

1 tablespoon olive oil

1 tablespoon orange juice

Zest of 1 orange

1 tablespoon fresh dill or 1 teaspoon dried

Salt and pepper to taste

1. Preheat oven to 400°F.
2. Cut a 18" piece of parchment.
3. Line a baking sheet with aluminum foil.
4. Slice carrots into coins ¼" thick.
5. Pour olive oil and orange juice over carrots.
6. Zest the orange over them, sprinkle with dill, and salt and pepper to taste.
7. Fold the parchment and place on a foil-covered baking sheet.
8. Bake for 20 minutes.

Calories: 37 | Fat: 3.5 g | Protein: 0 g | Sodium: 12 mg | Carbohydrates: 1.5 g | Fiber: 0.5 g

Asian Cabbage

Serves 4

When cooked correctly, cabbage is tender, flavorful, and has no odor. This isn't your grandma's cooked cabbage! Mix leftover cabbage with rice and tamari for an Asian encore.

½ head savoy cabbage

8 drops sesame oil

2 tablespoons stir-fry sauce

1. Preheat oven to 400°F.
2. Cut a 20" piece of parchment.
3. Line a baking sheet with aluminum foil.
4. Remove the hard center section of the cabbage.
5. Slice the cabbage thinly.
6. Place the cabbage in the center of the parchment paper.
7. Sprinkle the sesame oil over the cabbage, then the stir-fry sauce.
8. Gently toss the cabbage to mix.
9. Fold the parchment.
10. Bake for 15 minutes.

Savoy cabbage is crinkly and prettier than regular cabbage, but you can substitute any variety of cabbage you have on hand. Add more life to this dish with sesame seeds, sunflower seeds, or peanuts—your choice!

Calories: 40 | Fat: 1.5 g | Protein: 1 g | Sodium: 133 mg | Carbohydrates: 6.5 g | Fiber: 2 g

Asparagus with Creamy Mustard Sauce

Serves 4

Asparagus holds a special place in my heart, particularly when it is one of the first local vegetables available after the long winter. The sauce on this gives the asparagus a rich, creamy accompaniment that screams spring!

1 bunch asparagus

¼ cup light sour cream

1½ teaspoons mustard (I use a stone-ground mustard, but Dijon also works)

1 teaspoon fresh lemon juice

Salt and pepper to taste

1. Preheat oven to 400ºF.
2. Cut a 20" piece of parchment.
3. Line a baking sheet with aluminum foil.
4. Place asparagus on parchment.
5. Mix the other ingredients in a small bowl or custard cup and spread over asparagus.
6. Fold the parchment.
7. Bake for 20 minutes.

Calories: 37 | Fat: 2 g | Protein: 2 g | Sodium: 13 mg | Carbohydrates: 2.5 g | Fiber: 1 g

Roasted Carrots, Parsnip, and Rutabaga with Birch Syrup

Serves 4

Birch syrup makes another appearance here. If you opt for maple syrup instead, use only 1 tablespoon. Prepare this when you're feeling blue—the vibrancy of the vegetables on your plate should turn your mood!

12 baby carrots or 4 whole carrots, peeled

¼ rutabaga

1 parsnip

2 tablespoons birch syrup

Salt and pepper to taste

¼ teaspoon apple cider vinegar

1. Preheat oven to 400°F.
2. Cut a 20" piece of parchment.
3. Line a baking sheet with aluminum foil.
4. Slice the carrots as thinly as possible.
5. Cut off very, very thin rounds of rutabaga and cut the skin off.
6. Cut rutabaga into bite-size pieces.
7. Peel the parsnip and cut into very thin rounds.
8. Place all the vegetables on parchment.
9. Drizzle the birch syrup on top.
10. Season with salt and pepper.
11. Drizzle the vinegar over top.
12. Using a fork or your hands, lightly toss all the ingredients together.
13. Fold up the parchment.
14. Bake for 40 minutes.

Calories: 109 | Fat: 0.5 g | Protein: 1.5 g | Sodium: 52 mg | Carbohydrates: 26 g | Fiber: 6 g

Broccoli with Ginger, Lime, and Honey

Serves 4

Broccoli shakes its dull reputation with this bright dish. The unexpected flavors of ginger, lime, and honey make it come alive. This is even easier than boiling or steaming your broccoli since you have no pot to clean!

2 heads broccoli, cut into florets

½ tablespoon olive oil

1 teaspoon apple cider vinegar

2 teaspoons honey

⅛ teaspoon dried ginger

½ teaspoon lime juice

Salt and pepper to taste

2 teaspoons toasted sunflower seeds

1. Preheat oven to 400°F.
2. Cut a 20" piece of parchment.
3. Line a baking sheet with aluminum foil.
4. Place the broccoli on the parchment.
5. Mix everything else but the sunflower seeds in a small bowl and drizzle over the broccoli.
6. Fold the parchment.
7. Bake for 20 minutes.
8. Open the packet and sprinkle the seeds on top.

Calories: 140 | Fat: 3.5 g | Protein: 9 g | Sodium: 103 mg | Carbohydrates: 25 g | Fiber: 9.5 g

Snap Peas with Tzatziki

Serves 4

Tzatziki is a sauce made with Greek yogurt, lemon juice, and cucumber. You can make your own (see the sauce for Greek Lamb Meatball Pitas, Chapter 3) or buy it prepared at the supermarket. It's traditionally used as a cold dressing or dip, but in this recipe, you cook it with the peas, which results in a thick and creamy sauce.

2 cups snap peas

2 tablespoons tzatziki sauce

Salt and pepper to taste

1. Preheat oven to 400°F.
2. Cut a 20" piece of parchment.
3. Line a baking sheet with aluminum foil.
4. Place ingredients on the parchment and mix together.
5. Fold the parchment.
6. Bake for 15 minutes.

Calories: 34 | Fat: 0 g | Protein: 2 g | Sodium: 5 mg | Carbohydrates: 5 g | Fiber: 2 g

Spinach Artichoke Pie

Serves 4–6

As an hors d'oeuvre, cut into small squares, this can't be beat. But you can also serve it as a side dish to a bowl of soup. Got leftovers? Enjoy them at room temperature or heat them up in the toaster oven.

1 refrigerated unbaked pie crust

10 ounces chopped frozen spinach, defrosted and squeezed dry

1 13-ounce can artichoke hearts, drained and chopped

¼ cup light mayonnaise

¼ cup shredded fontina cheese

2 cloves garlic, chopped

¼ cup shredded part-skim mozzarella cheese

½ teaspoon fresh lemon juice

Salt and pepper to taste

½ cup light chive and onion cream cheese, softened

1. Preheat oven to 400ºF.

2. Cut a 20" piece of parchment.

3. Line a baking sheet with aluminum foil.

4. Place the pie crust on the parchment and scrunch up the edges to make a 6" × 6" square, keeping the edges up to create a border.

5. In a small bowl mix all the other ingredients.

6. Spread the mixture evenly over the pie crust.

7. Without folding the parchment paper, bake for 25 minutes.

Calories: 268 | Fat: 19 g | Protein: 6 g | Sodium: 515 mg | Carbohydrates: 22 g | Fiber: 1.5 g

Swiss Chard with Butter and Balsamic

Serves 2

The color of this dish makes me so happy. And the balsamic vinegar provides a tangy flavor note.

1 bunch Swiss chard (leaves and stems)

2 tablespoons butter

1 tablespoon balsamic vinegar

Salt and pepper to taste

1. Preheat oven to 400°F.

2. Cut a very large piece of parchment for this—at least 36". (When you mound the Swiss chard, it's easier to wrangle with a bigger piece!)

3. Line a baking sheet with aluminum foil.

4. Roughly chop the chard, or rip it into pieces with your hands.

5. Place the chard on the parchment.

6. Dot with pieces of the butter.

7. Sprinkle the balsamic around, and then season with salt and pepper.

8. Fold the parchment.

9. Bake for 20 minutes.

Swiss chard comes in many colors. Whether you use red or white chard, you'll be greeted with deep green contrasted with red or white when you open the packet.

Calories: 119 | Fat: 12 g | Protein: 1.5 g | Sodium: 231 mg | Carbohydrates: 4 g | Fiber: 1 g

Brussels Sprouts with Pumpkin Seed Oil and Pecans

Serves 4

My husband does not love Brussels sprouts, but I adore them, so I am always looking for new ways to entice him to like them. This recipe did just that. Try serving this dish on Thanksgiving—it pairs wonderfully with turkey and all the trimmings. Feel free to leave out nuts if you don't care for them.

¾ pound Brussels sprouts, trimmed and cut in half (in quarters if very large)

1 tablespoon pumpkin seed oil

Salt and pepper to taste

¼ cup finely chopped pecans

1 tablespoon butter

1. Preheat oven to 400°F.

2. Cut a 20" piece of parchment.

3. Line a baking sheet with aluminum foil.

4. Place the sprouts on the parchment.

5. Drizzle with the pumpkin seed oil.

6. Season with salt and pepper, and lightly toss.

7. Fold the parchment.

8. Bake for 30 minutes.

9. Place the pecans and butter in a small glass bowl and microwave, stirring frequently, for 1 minute.

10. Remove packet from the oven and carefully open it.

11. Drizzle butter-pecan mixture over the Brussels sprouts.

12. Return to the oven and broil for 1–2 minutes or until the sprouts start to lightly brown.

You can find pumpkin seed oil (which imparts a light, nutty flavor to this dish) in the grocery store with other specialty oils, like walnut and hazelnut. However, if you can't find it, substitute a good extra-virgin olive oil.

Calories: 136 | Fat: 12 g | Protein: 3 g | Sodium: 47 mg | Carbohydrates: 8.6 g | Fiber: 3 g

Hot Asian Carrot Peanut Slaw

Serves 4

In the summer I make a cold carrot salad, but I've modified it for this hot nutty-sweet slaw. Cooking the dish softens the carrots and releases the vegetable's juices. Pair that with warmed peanut butter and Asian flavorings and you get a recipe worth dog-earing.

1¼ cups shredded carrots

½ cup creamy peanut butter

1 tablespoon rice vinegar

1 teaspoon tamari or soy sauce

1 teaspoon brown sugar

Ground black pepper to taste

⅛ cup shredded fresh parsley

1. Preheat oven to 400°F.

2. Cut a 20" piece of parchment.

3. Line a baking sheet with aluminum foil.

4. Place the carrots on parchment.

5. Place the peanut butter in a glass bowl or measuring cup and microwave on High for 30 seconds.

6. Stir in rice vinegar, tamari or soy sauce, brown sugar, some ground pepper, and the chopped parsley.

7. Pour over carrots and use your hands or a fork to toss together.

8. Fold the parchment.

9. Bake for 40 minutes.

When I use fresh parsley in a dish like this I often just rip it up into small pieces with my hands, instead of using a knife to chop it. There's less mess and I enjoy the smell of the fresh herb in my hands.

Calories: 224 | Fat: 16 g | Protein: 9 g | Sodium: 139 mg | Carbohydrates: 15 g | Fiber: 4 g

Green Beans with Mushrooms

Serves 2 or 3

Mushrooms add a new depth to green beans, making them feel heartier and more filling. The Worcestershire sauce also bumps up the richness factor in this easy-to-execute dish.

¾ pound green beans, trimmed

5 or 6 white or Baby Bella mushrooms, sliced

⅛ teaspoon onion powder

1 teaspoon olive oil

1 tablespoon Worcestershire sauce

Salt and pepper to taste

1. Preheat oven to 400°F.

2. Cut a 20" piece of parchment.

3. Line a baking sheet with aluminum foil.

4. Toss the ingredients together on the parchment.

5. Fold the parchment.

6. Bake for 35 minutes.

Calories: 43 | Fat: 1.5 g | Protein: 1.5 g | Sodium: 60 mg | Carbohydrates: 6.5 g | Fiber: 2 g

"Stuffed" Artichokes

Serves 4

Whole artichokes seem to intimidate many. It's no wonder: they need to be trimmed and boiled for a long time before you can enjoy them. And stuffing an artichoke takes time and patience. This no-pot solution gives you everything you love about stuffed artichokes with none of the fuss.

12 ounces frozen artichoke hearts (quartered)

4 tablespoons butter (cut into small pieces)

⅛ teaspoon garlic powder

1 tablespoon lemon juice

¼ cup Parmesan cheese (reserve 2 tablespoons)

¼ cup chopped parsley

Salt and pepper to taste

1. Preheat oven to 400°F.
2. Cut a 20" piece of parchment.
3. Line a baking sheet with aluminum foil.
4. Place all ingredients except the reserved Parmesan on the parchment.
5. Lightly toss them together.
6. Fold the parchment.
7. Bake for 30 minutes.
8. Open the parchment and sprinkle artichokes with reserved cheese. Leaving the packet open, return to the oven for about 12 minutes.

Calories: 163 | Fat: 14 g | Protein: 5 g | Sodium: 255 mg | Carbohydrates: 7.5 g | Fiber: 3.5 g

Zucchini with Bean Sprouts

Serves 2

In the summer when zucchini rules the garden and the farm stand, I'm always on the hunt for ways to use it up. This quick recipe does just that in a fresh and tasty way.

1 small zucchini, thinly sliced

½ cup bean sprouts

1 tablespoon fresh parsley, chopped

7 drops sesame oil

¾ tablespoon tamari or soy sauce

1. Preheat oven to 400°F.
2. Cut a 20" piece of parchment.
3. Line a baking sheet with aluminum foil.
4. Place all the ingredients on the parchment and toss with your hands or a fork.
5. Fold the parchment.
6. Bake for 15 minutes.

Calories: 34 | Fat: 2 g | Protein: 2 g | Sodium: 377 mg | Carbohydrates: 2 g | Fiber: 1 g

Herbed Corn on the Cob

Serves 1

Cooking corn on the cob this way, with goat cheese and cilantro, results in a veggie side that you won't be able to stop eating! Substitute basil for cilantro if you prefer, or queso fresco for the goat cheese. Or, try it with a wedge of Laughing Cow cheese (any flavor) rubbed over it.

1 tablespoon butter

1 tablespoon goat cheese

1 tablespoon fresh cilantro, chopped

Salt and pepper to taste

1 ear of corn, husked

1. Preheat oven to 400°F.
2. Cut a 12" piece of parchment.
3. Line a baking sheet with aluminum foil.
4. Melt the butter in a small glass bowl in the microwave.
5. Add the goat cheese and return to microwave for about 10 more seconds.
6. Stir, then add cilantro, salt, and pepper.
7. Spread mixture over the corn.
8. Fold the parchment.
9. Bake for 15 minutes.

> This dish also tastes great when cooked on an outdoor grill. Just be sure to wrap the corn in foil instead of parchment paper and turn the packet once. Cooking time will depend on the heat of your grill, but plan on about the same time frame.

Calories: 276 | Fat: 17 g | Protein: 7.5 g | Sodium: 197 mg | Carbohydrates: 30 g | Fiber: 3.5 g

Spinach, Corn, and Cherry Tomatoes

Serves 4

In the summer, enjoy this heavenly dish made with fresh corn cut off the cob and ripe tomatoes. Or, make it in the winter with frozen corn as a reminder of warmer days. Add 3 tablespoons of feta cheese for a tangy variation.

5 ounces baby spinach

1 cup corn

½ pint cherry tomatoes, cut in half

2 tablespoons fresh basil (substitute 1 tablespoon dry if needed)

2 teaspoons balsamic vinegar

1 tablespoon olive oil

Salt and pepper to taste

1. Preheat oven to 400°F.
2. Cut a 20" piece of parchment.
3. Line a baking sheet with aluminum foil.
4. Place the spinach on the parchment and top with corn and tomatoes.
5. Sprinkle with basil, balsamic, and oil.
6. Season with salt and pepper.
7. Lightly toss all ingredients.
8. Fold the parchment.
9. Bake for 15 minutes.
10. Open the packet and bake for 5 more minutes.

Calories: 87 | Fat: 4 g | Protein: 3 g | Sodium: 34 mg | Carbohydrates: 13 g | Fiber: 2.5 g

Roasted Parmesan Broccoli and Cauliflower

Serves 4

Dress up your veggies by adding some Parmesan cheese for instant flavor. Mixing broccoli and cauliflower in this dish also adds visual interest.

2 small heads or 1 large head broccoli, cut into small florets

½ head cauliflower, cut into small florets

2 tablespoons olive oil

¼ cup Parmesan cheese

1. Preheat oven to 400°F.

2. Cut a 20" piece of parchment.

3. Line a baking sheet with aluminum foil.

4. Place the broccoli and cauliflower florets on the parchment paper.

5. Drizzle with olive oil.

6. Fold parchment.

7. Bake for 25 minutes.

8. Open packet, fold the sides down or cut them off, and sprinkle with Parmesan cheese.

9. Bake another 5 minutes, then broil for 5 minutes.

Calories: 159 | Fat: 9 g | Protein: 9 g | Sodium: 170 mg | Carbohydrates: 11 g | Fiber: 7 g

Broccolini with Brown Butter and Cashews

Serves 4

Broccolini, also called baby broccoli, has a slightly sweet flavor with notes of broccoli and asparagus. If you don't like to eat a lot of stems, trim them down before cooking. The cashews and brown butter bring a touch of sweetness to the dish.

6 tablespoons butter

1 medium bunch broccolini

Salt and pepper to taste

½ cup honey-roasted cashews

1. Preheat oven to 400°F.

2. Cut a 20" piece of parchment.

3. Line a baking sheet with aluminum foil.

4. Brown the butter in a small glass bowl in the microwave (it will have a delicious, nutty aroma when it's brown, but don't let it get past brown to black!).

5. Place the broccolini on the parchment.

6. Drizzle the butter over the broccolini. Season with salt and pepper.

7. Fold the parchment.

8. Bake for 20 minutes.

9. Open the packet, sprinkle the cashews on top, and serve.

Calories: 256 | Fat: 24 g | Protein: 6 g | Sodium: 215 mg | Carbohydrates: 8 g | Fiber: 4 g

Open Sesame Asparagus

Serves 4

Asparagus tastes delicious when roasted in the oven; the flavor deepens and it tastes a bit nutty. The light sesame flavor adds even more interest and nutty flavor without overpowering the asparagus.

1 bunch asparagus, trimmed

½ tablespoon olive oil

½ teaspoon sesame oil

1 tablespoon soy sauce

¼ teaspoon toasted sesame seeds

1. Preheat oven to 400°F.
2. Cut a 20" piece of parchment.
3. Line a baking sheet with aluminum foil.
4. Place the asparagus in the center of a sheet of parchment.
5. Drizzle with oils and soy sauce.
6. Sprinkle with the seeds.
7. Fold the parchment
8. Bake for 15 minutes.
9. Remove from oven and allow to rest for about 5 minutes before serving.

Calories: 31 | Fat: 2.5 g | Protein: 1.5 g | Sodium: 231 mg | Carbohydrates: 1.5 g | Fiber: 1 g

Honey Dill Carrots

Serves 4

Kids love matchstick carrots—they look like confetti! The dill and honey in this dish impart a slightly sweet-tangy flavor that awakens the palate.

1¼ cups shredded or matchstick carrots

1½ tablespoons honey

½ teaspoon dried dill

1 tablespoon butter

Salt and pepper to taste

1. Preheat oven to 400°F.
2. Cut a 20" piece of parchment.
3. Line a baking sheet with aluminum foil.
4. Place the carrots in the center of the parchment paper.
5. Drizzle with the honey.
6. Sprinkle the dill over them.
7. Dot with the butter.
8. Season with salt and pepper.
9. Fold the parchment.
10. Bake for 40 minutes.

Calories: 79 | Fat: 3 g | Protein: 1 g | Sodium: 79 mg | Carbohydrates: 14 g | Fiber: 2 g

Peas with Onion, Scallions, and Ham

Serves 4

Add a few simple ingredients to a bowl of plain old peas and you've suddenly got an interesting dish everyone wants to try. For more kick, substitute salami for the ham.

2 cups frozen peas

1 tablespoon butter

1 tablespoon chopped onion

1 tablespoon chopped scallions, green and white parts

1 slice ham, chopped

Salt and pepper to taste

1. Preheat oven to 400ºF.

2. Cut a 20" piece of parchment.

3. Line a baking sheet with aluminum foil.

4. Place the peas on the parchment.

5. Place the butter and chopped onion in a small glass bowl and microwave for 1 minute.

6. Pour onion mixture over the peas.

7. Add the scallions and ham and season with salt and pepper.

8. Fold the parchment.

9. Bake for 25 minutes.

Calories: 103 | Fat: 5 g | Protein: 4.5 g | Sodium: 176 mg | Carbohydrates: 10 g | Fiber: 3 g

Stuffed Portobellos

Serves 1

Try adding a slice of prosciutto to this for a different flavor. These are delicious as a vegetarian main course, but also go nicely with steak. For lunch, sandwich the cooked portobello inside a bun or pita.

1 portobello mushroom, cleaned and stem removed

Salt and pepper to taste

¼ cup defrosted and squeezed dry frozen chopped spinach

1 tablespoon goat cheese

Pinch Italian seasoning

Pinch garlic salt

¼ teaspoon steak sauce (such as A.1. brand)

1. Preheat oven to 400°F.
2. Cut a 12" piece of parchment.
3. Line a baking sheet with aluminum foil.
4. Place the portobello on the parchment.
5. Season with salt and pepper.
6. Spread the spinach on top and crumble goat cheese over it.
7. Sprinkle on Italian seasoning and garlic salt.
8. Drizzle steak sauce on top.
9. Fold the parchment.
10. Bake for 15 minutes.

Portobello mushrooms are big and have a satisfying meaty texture. In this dish they stand well on their own as a main dish, but they can be used as a side dish as well.

Calories: 95 | Fat: 5 g | Protein: 7.5 g | Sodium: 123 mg | Carbohydrates: 8 g | Fiber: 3 g

Baked Brie

Serves 6–8

This makes a delicious lunch when paired with a fresh green salad. Or, serve the brie with some French bread for a decadent appetizer. Either way, you can easily reheat any leftovers (although I wouldn't count on any)!

2 tablespoons butter

½ cup sliced almonds

1 8-ounce brie wheel

1. Preheat oven to 400°F.
2. Cut a 12" piece of parchment.
3. Line a baking sheet with aluminum foil.
4. Place the butter and almonds in a small glass bowl and microwave about 1 minute.
5. Place the brie on the parchment.
6. Pour the butter and nuts on top of the brie.
7. Fold the parchment.
8. Bake for 15 minutes.

Calories: 153 | Fat: 14 g | Protein: 7 g | Sodium: 208 mg | Carbohydrates: 1 g | Fiber: 0.5 g

Beans and Greens

Serves 2

Serve this with bread and fresh fruit, such as cherries or sliced apples, and you've got yourself a satisfying meal. It also pairs well with Baked Brie (see previous recipe). Sometimes I sprinkle some Parmesan cheese on top to dress things up.

1 tablespoon olive oil

2 cloves garlic, chopped

7 ounces escarole (half a bag)

1 can cannellini beans, drained and rinsed

¼ teaspoon red pepper flakes

Salt and pepper to taste

1. Preheat oven to 400ºF.

2. Cut a 20" piece of parchment.

3. Line a baking sheet with aluminum foil.

4. Place olive oil and garlic in a small glass bowl and microwave for about 20 seconds.

5. Place escarole on parchment.

6. Top with beans.

7. Drizzle olive oil and garlic over the vegetables, sprinkle with red pepper, and season with salt and pepper.

8. Toss everything together.

9. Fold the parchment.

10. Bake for 20 minutes.

11. Toss again before serving.

Calories: 223 | Fat: 7 g | Protein: 9 g | Sodium: 24 mg | Carbohydrates: 32 g | Fiber: 8 g

Cauliflower and Sweet Potato Curry

Serves 2

I use white sweet potatoes in this recipe, but you can substitute the orange variety if you prefer a more moist and sweet dish. The end result after cooking is a rich, vibrant, lovely yellow color thanks to the turmeric and curry powder.

½ large white sweet potato, peeled and cut into ½" slices, then quartered

¼ large head of cauliflower, cut into florets and halved

⅓ cup matchstick carrots

¼ teaspoon curry powder

¼ teaspoon turmeric

¼ teaspoon cumin

⅛ teaspoon garlic powder

⅛ teaspoon dry ginger

Salt and pepper to taste

1 tablespoon chopped onion

2 tablespoons olive oil

2 tablespoons chicken broth

1. Preheat oven to 400°F.

2. Cut a 20" piece of parchment.

3. Line a baking sheet with aluminum foil.

4. Place the potatoes, cauliflower, and carrots on the parchment.

5. Add all the remaining ingredients.

6. Toss the ingredients together.

7. Fold the parchment.

8. Bake for 25 minutes.

9. Toss again before serving.

Calories: 183 | Fat: 14 g | Protein: 3 g | Sodium: 97 mg | Carbohydrates: 14 g | Fiber: 4.5 g

Succotash

Serves 2

A popular Southern side dish, succotash has a texture that makes it seem rich, but most of that texture is due to the creamed corn—and not to a lot of cream. Pimiento can be used in place of the red bell pepper if you have some leftover from other recipes you want to use up. It will just have a softer texture in the dish.

1 cup frozen lima beans

½ cup frozen corn

½ cup canned creamed corn

1 tablespoon melted butter

1 tablespoon skim milk

½ teaspoon sugar

1 teaspoon cornstarch

¼ red bell pepper, diced

Salt and pepper to taste

1. Preheat oven to 400°F.
2. Cut a 20" piece of parchment.
3. Line a baking sheet with aluminum foil.
4. Place lima beans, frozen corn, and creamed corn on parchment.
5. In a small bowl, mix butter, milk, sugar, and cornstarch.
6. Pour mixture over the vegetables.
7. Add the bell pepper and salt and pepper.
8. Fold the parchment.
9. Bake for 30 minutes.

Calories: 257 | Fat: 7 g | Protein: 9 g | Sodium: 109 mg | Carbohydrates: 44 g | Fiber: 7 g

Asparagus with Mushrooms and Fava Beans

Serves 4

Fava beans are a great way to add some protein to your veggie dishes. Serve this as a side dish or as a vegetarian entrée. Chicken broth can be used in place of veggie broth if you're not feeding vegetarians.

1 19-ounce can fava beans, drained and rinsed

10 white or Baby Bella mushrooms, sliced thinly

1 bunch asparagus, bottoms cut off and cut into 1"–2" pieces

2 tablespoons white wine

2 tablespoons vegetable broth

1 tablespoon olive oil

2 cloves garlic, chopped

Salt and pepper to taste

1 tablespoon panko bread crumbs

1. Preheat oven to 400°F.

2. Cut a 20" piece of parchment.

3. Line a baking sheet with aluminum foil.

4. Place asparagus on parchment and top with wine, broth, and oil.

5. Top with garlic and salt and pepper and gently toss with your hands or a spoon to combine.

6. Fold the parchment.

7. Bake for 22 minutes, until asparagus is tender.

8. Open parchment.

9. Top with panko and spray with cooking spray.

10. Broil for 2 minutes.

Calories: 178 | Fat: 7 g | Protein: 9 g | Sodium: 534 mg | Carbohydrates: 20 g | Fiber: 6.5 g

Roasted Kohlrabi

Serves 2

Looking for a veggie dish that's new and different? Give this one a try. Kohlrabi comes in purple or green varieties and is a farmers' market darling. Seek out some super-fresh bulbs and get cooking!

2 kohlrabi

1 teaspoon lemon juice

1 tablespoon melted butter

1 tablespoon cream

Salt and pepper to taste

1 tablespoon fresh parsley, chopped

1. Preheat oven to 400°F.
2. Cut a 20" piece of parchment.
3. Line a baking sheet with aluminum foil.
4. Cut the stems off the kohlrabi, then cut the ends off.
5. Use a knife to cut away the outer skin.
6. Slice thinly and then quarter each slice.
7. Place on the parchment.
8. Drizzle with lemon juice, butter, and cream.
9. Season with salt and pepper and sprinkle with parsley.
10. Fold the parchment.
11. Bake for 45 minutes or until tender.

Kohlrabi is a bit strange looking, and it's sometimes described as a cross between a turnip and a cabbage, but that's not the case. It is in the brassica family and has a mild taste reminiscent of rutabaga with cabbage undernotes. Select small kohlrabi no larger than $2\frac{1}{2}$" in diameter, with the leaves still attached.

Calories: 88 | Fat: 7 g | Protein: 2 g | Sodium: 79 mg | Carbohydrates: 5.5 g | Fiber: 3 g

Creamy Leeks and Carrots

Serves 2

Leeks become smooth, creamy, and fragrant when slowly cooked with milk and butter, and in this dish the carrots provide a pop of color. Feel free to substitute other cheeses in this recipe.

2 leeks

1 cup matchstick carrots

1 tablespoon butter

1 teaspoon olive oil

Salt and pepper to taste

2 tablespoons skim milk

1 teaspoon cornstarch

1 slice reduced-fat Swiss cheese, torn or finely sliced

1. Preheat oven to 350°F.
2. Cut a 20" piece of parchment.
3. Line a baking sheet with aluminum foil.
4. Cut the dark green ends off the leeks and remove the roots.
5. Cut the leeks in half and wash well, getting between the layers to remove dirt.
6. Slice thinly and place on parchment.
7. Add carrots and toss.
8. Melt butter in a small glass bowl in the microwave, being careful not to burn.
9. Drizzle butter and olive oil on top of leek-carrot mixture. Season with salt and pepper.
10. In a small bowl mix milk and cornstarch and drizzle over the top.
11. Fold the parchment.
12. Bake for 45 minutes.
13. Open the packet, toss ingredients, and sprinkle cheese on top.
14. Return to oven with packet open for 5 minutes.

Calories: 188 | Fat: 9 g | Protein: 7 g | Sodium: 166 mg | Carbohydrates: 22 g | Fiber: 4 g

Asparagus with Blue Cheese

Serves 4

Asparagus was once available only in the spring, but now that you can get asparagus grown in California or Peru year round, it's good to have a variety of recipes on hand for when the craving strikes. Pungent blue cheese dressing bathes the asparagus in this easy side dish.

1 bunch asparagus, trimmed

¼ cup light blue cheese dressing

Salt and pepper to taste

1. Preheat oven to 400°F.
2. Cut a 20" piece of parchment.
3. Line a baking sheet with aluminum foil.
4. Place the asparagus on the parchment. Drizzle the dressing over it, and season with salt and pepper.
5. Fold the parchment.
6. Bake for 20 minutes.

Calories: 57 | Fat: 2 g | Protein: 1.5 g | Sodium: 111 mg | Carbohydrates: 3.5 g | Fiber: 1 g

Green Beans with Dates and Walnuts

Serves 4

The dates melt a bit while this cooks and coat the beans to create a deeply flavorful veggie dish. The sweetness of this dish makes me feel like I'm having a little bit of dessert with my main course! I like this served alongside steak, especially in the winter when I'm craving something warm and hearty.

½ pound green beans, trimmed

¼ cup dates, chopped

¼ cup walnuts, chopped

1 tablespoon olive oil

Salt and pepper to taste

1. Preheat oven to 400ºF.

2. Cut a 20" piece of parchment.

3. Line a baking sheet with aluminum foil.

4. Place the beans on the parchment.

5. Top with dates, nuts, oil, salt, and pepper.

6. Toss to coat.

7. Fold the parchment.

8. Bake for 30 minutes.

Calories: 164 | Fat: 8 g | Protein: 2.5 g | Sodium: 2 mg | Carbohydrates: 23 g | Fiber: 4 g

Summer Squash Mix-Up

Serves 4

This is based on my mom's summer squash casserole, which she makes at least once a summer when she's just tired of plain old squash. Look no further for the perfect solution to use up the overabundance of squash and tomatoes you may be faced with when your garden is in full bloom.

1 medium zucchini

1 medium yellow squash

½ cup cherry tomatoes

½ cup onion, thinly sliced, then roughly chopped

1 tablespoon Italian seasoning

Salt and pepper to taste

2 tablespoons beef broth

1 tablespoon olive oil

2–3 tablespoons Parmesan cheese

1. Preheat oven to 400°F.
2. Cut a 20" piece of parchment.
3. Line a baking sheet with aluminum foil.
4. Thinly slice the zucchini and squash.
5. Halve the cherry tomatoes.
6. Place them all on the parchment.
7. Add onions, Italian seasoning, salt, and pepper.
8. Drizzle on broth and olive oil.
9. Toss everything together to coat.
10. Fold the parchment.
11. Bake for 30 minutes.
12. Open the packet, sprinkle on the cheese, and broil for 2 minutes.

Calories: 68 | Fat: 4.5 g | Protein: 2.5 g | Sodium: 80 mg | Carbohydrates: 3.5 g | Fiber: 1 g

Orange Pistachio Broccoli

Serves 4

Pistachios, orange juice, and garlic powder give broccoli a fun kick in this side dish. A wonderful accompaniment to grilled fish! If you don't have pistachios, try using hazelnuts for an unexpected taste twist.

1 large head broccoli, cut into florets

¼ cup orange juice

1 tablespoon cornstarch

⅛ teaspoon garlic powder

⅓ cup shelled pistachios

Pepper

Salt (only if the pistachios are unsalted)

1. Preheat oven to 400°F.
2. Cut a 20" piece of parchment.
3. Line a baking sheet with aluminum foil.
4. Place the broccoli florets on parchment.
5. Mix orange juice with cornstarch in a small bowl and drizzle over broccoli.
6. Dust with garlic powder.
7. Sprinkle the pistachios on top and season with pepper and salt if needed.
8. Fold the parchment.
9. Bake for 22 minutes.

Calories: 102 | Fat: 5 g | Protein: 5 g | Sodium: 30 mg | Carbohydrates: 13 g | Fiber: 4 g

Baked Goat Cheese with Pesto and Sun-Dried Tomatoes

Serves 2

Serve this as a fun appetizer or with a big salad for a complete meal. Leftovers are great on sandwiches or mixed into some piping-hot whole-grain pasta.

4 ounces goat cheese

1 tablespoon pesto (homemade or jarred)

1 tablespoon chopped sun-dried tomatoes

Pinch red pepper flakes

Whole-grain crackers or bread

1. Preheat oven to 400°F.
2. Cut a 20" piece of parchment.
3. Line a baking sheet with aluminum foil.
4. Spray the parchment with cooking spray.
5. Place the goat cheese on the parchment.
6. Top with pesto, tomatoes, and red pepper flakes.
7. Fold the parchment.
8. Bake for 15 minutes.
9. Serve alongside crackers or bread.

Calories: 316 | Fat: 23 g | Protein: 16 g | Sodium: 449 mg | Carbohydrates: 16 g | Fiber: 2.5 g

Savory Napoleon

Serves 8

I love this dish because it's akin to an easy, modern spanakopita. This makes a phe-nomenal appetizer or vegetarian entrée. The filo tends to crumble a bit when you cut it into squares, but that has no impact on the amazing flavor.

5 ounces Baby Bella or white mush-rooms, chopped

5 ounces frozen spinach, defrosted and squeezed dry

1 teaspoon Dijon mustard

Salt and pepper to taste

½ tablespoon olive oil

1 teaspoon fresh lemon juice

¼ teaspoon red pepper

2 tablespoons plain low-fat or nonfat yogurt

1 tablespoon blue cheese

4 ounces shredded Monterey jack cheese with an additional 1 ounce reserved for topping

6 sheets filo dough

Nonstick cooking spray

1. Preheat oven to 400°F.

2. Line a baking sheet with aluminum foil, then parchment.

3. In a medium bowl, mix all ingredients except filo and cooking spray.

4. Lay 3 sheets of filo in a stack on the parchment.

5. Spray half of the top filo sheet with cooking spray, leaving the other half of the stack unsprayed to fold over later. Top the sprayed half with ⅓ of the mushroom mixture.

6. Fold the other half over on top of it. Spray the top of the filo with cooking spray. Top with ⅓ of the mixture.

7. Place the remaining 3 filo sheets on top, so half is on top of the ones already prepared. Spray half of the top sheet with cooking spray.

8. Spread remaining ⅓ of the mixture onto the sprayed half of the filo.

9. Fold remaining half over. Spray top with cooking spray. Top with a sprinkle of additional Monterey jack cheese.

10. Bake with parchment open for 12 minutes.

Calories: 196 | Fat: 14 g | Protein: 6.5 g | Sodium: 172 mg | Carbohydrates: 11 g | Fiber: 1 g

Baked Mixed Greens

Serves 2

This mix of various greens gets a spicy-sweet jolt from the fennel and orange juice. If you have other greens on hand, such as Swiss chard or collards, feel free to swap them in. Cooking greens in parchment makes it a breeze to get the health benefits without much effort.

1 cup tightly packed escarole, chopped

1 cup tightly packed kale, chopped

1 cup tightly packed baby spinach

½ cup chopped fennel bulb

1 tablespoon olive oil

1 teaspoon red wine vinegar

1 tablespoon orange juice

Salt and pepper to taste

1. Preheat oven to 400°F.

2. Cut a 20" piece of parchment.

3. Line a baking sheet with aluminum foil.

4. Place all the greens and fennel on the parchment.

5. Drizzle on olive oil, vinegar, and orange juice and season with salt and pepper.

6. Toss the ingredients.

7. Fold the parchment.

8. Bake for 20 minutes.

Calories: 101 | Fat: 7 g | Protein: 2 g | Sodium: 47 mg | Carbohydrates: 9 g | Fiber: 2.5 g

Roasted Garlic

Serves 2

When you roast a head of garlic it caramelizes and becomes mild. There are myriad uses for this delicious spread, but I am partial to slathering it on a warm hunk of French bread. Reheat leftovers or mix into a pasta dish for a flavor infusion.

1 head garlic

1 teaspoon olive oil

1. Preheat oven to 400°F.
2. Cut a 12" piece of parchment.
3. Line a baking sheet with aluminum foil.
4. Cut the top off the garlic head, but do not peel the garlic.
5. Place on the parchment.
6. Drizzle with olive oil.
7. Fold the parchment.
8. Bake for 1 hour.
9. When cool enough to handle, squeeze warm garlic out of the individual cloves into a small bowl. Spread before it cools.

Calories: 45 | Fat: 2.5 g | Protein: 1 g | Sodium: 3 mg | Carbohydrates: 5.5 g | Fiber: 0.5 g

CHAPTER 7

Bread, Rice, and Potato Dishes

Potato and rice pots tend to be quite sticky. With these recipes you'll be able to serve up tasty side dishes without any time spent scrubbing. You might not think these kinds of dishes would lend themselves to parchment paper cooking, but they turn out beautifully. Enjoy these dishes as accompaniments to the meat and seafood dishes in the book.

German Potatoes

Serves 4

German potato salad dishes can be sour, dry, and boring, but this reinvented recipe uses cream cheese and yogurt to keep it moist and has just enough vinegar to give it a kick. My husband asks for this dish over and over!

8–10 medium Yukon Gold potatoes

1 cup plain nonfat yogurt

2 tablespoons light cream cheese

8 teaspoons apple cider vinegar

2–4 slices of deli ham, cut into ½" pieces

Salt and pepper to taste

½ teaspoon caraway seeds

1. Preheat oven to 400°F.
2. Prepare this in two or four packets so cut either 18" or 24" of parchment paper.
3. Line a baking sheet with aluminum foil.
4. Cook the potatoes in the microwave on High for about 5 minutes, or until they are soft when pricked with a fork.
5. Allow them to cool enough to handle.
6. Remove skin using your hands or a knife.
7. Cut the potatoes into 1" chunks and place in a bowl.
8. Add yogurt, cream cheese, vinegar, ham, salt, and pepper.
9. Mix, being careful not to mash the potatoes.
10. Place the potatoes on the parchment paper.
11. Sprinkle with caraway seeds.
12. Fold the parchment.
13. Bake for 20 minutes.

Calories: 422 | Fat: 5 g | Protein: 14 g | Sodium: 225 mg | Carbohydrates: 82 g | Fiber: 7 g

Parmesan Rice

Serves 4

Although incredibly simple, this dish features the nutty flavor of brown butter, which gives it amazing depth. That, combined with the cheese, makes this one of my all-time favorites. It also reheats well in the microwave, so make plenty. Then you can serve it twice in one week!

½ stick butter

3 cups hot cooked brown rice (made in your rice cooker, or use instant brown rice cooked in the microwave according to package instructions)

Salt and pepper to taste

½ cup finely grated Parmesan cheese

1. Preheat oven to 400°F.

2. Line a baking sheet with foil and lay out two pieces of 18" parchment.

3. Melt the butter in a glass bowl in the microwave until it is brown.

4. Divide the rice between the two pieces of parchment. Flatten the rice into a 1"-thick square or circle on each piece.

5. Spoon the brown butter over the rice evenly.

6. Salt and pepper the rice.

7. Sprinkle cheese over the rice.

8. Fold the parchment.

9. Bake for 15 minutes.

Calories: 409 | Fat: 16 g | Protein: 7 g | Sodium: 312 mg | Carbohydrates: 17 g | Fiber: 1.5 g

Oliver's Spinach Bread

Serves 6–8

A local restaurant in my area is known for its decadent garlic bread, loaded with butter and spinach. This version packs lots of spinach along with the flavors of garlic and Parmesan cheese. Everyone will want seconds of this fragrant bread.

5 tablespoons butter

4 cloves garlic, minced

1 loaf batard bread (a flatter Italian bread will also work)

10 ounces frozen chopped spinach, defrosted and squeezed dry

¼ cup Parmesan cheese

Salt

1. Preheat oven to 400°F.

2. Cut a piece of parchment that is 2½ times the length of the bread.

3. Line a baking sheet with aluminum foil.

4. Place butter and garlic in a small glass bowl and microwave on high for 1 minute.

5. Slice the bread in half lengthwise, parallel to the countertop, so it is cut like a sandwich roll.

6. Spread the butter and garlic on both halves.

7. Place the spinach on the bottom half of the bread and top with the cheese. Sprinkle with salt.

8. Place the top half of the bread on the bottom half.

9. Fold the parchment.

10. Bake for 17 minutes. To serve, cut into 1½" slices.

Calories: 150 | Fat: 9 g | Protein: 4 g | Sodium: 289 mg | Carbohydrates: 15 g | Fiber: 1 g

Tortellini with Chicken and Pesto

Serves 2

Substitute ham for the chicken if you like, and frozen broccoli for the peas to try something different. And if you're feeling really adventurous, try different flavors of tortellini as well! (I'm partial to spinach.)

9 ounces refrigerated fresh tortellini

¼ cup frozen peas

1 boneless skinless chicken breast, cut into bite-size pieces

Salt and pepper to taste

¼ cup pesto

¼ teaspoon Italian seasoning or basil

2 tablespoons chicken broth

1 tablespoon olive oil

¼ cup Parmesan cheese

1. Preheat oven to 400°F.
2. Cut a 20" piece of parchment.
3. Line a baking sheet with aluminum foil.
4. Soak the tortellini in hot water for about 5 minutes.
5. Place the tortellini on a piece of parchment.
6. Spread the peas on top.
7. Add the chicken.
8. Season with salt and pepper.
9. Drop dollops of the pesto over the food.
10. Sprinkle with Italian seasoning. Drizzle with chicken broth and olive oil.
11. Sprinkle on Parmesan cheese.
12. Using a fork, gently mix and toss the ingredients together a bit so you no longer see large clumps of pesto.
13. Fold the parchment.
14. Bake for 20 minutes.

Calories: 773 | Fat: 41 g | Protein: 37 g | Sodium: 510 mg | Carbohydrates: 65 g | Fiber: 4 g

Herb and Garlic Bread

Serves 8

This is one of my mom's signature dishes, which she makes with herbs picked fresh from her garden. If you have fresh basil, oregano, or tarragon, definitely use those in lieu of the Italian seasoning mix. This dish goes with almost anything and makes a nice addition to any dinner party menu.

5 tablespoons butter

2 cloves garlic, chopped

1 tablespoon Italian herb mix or 2–3 tablespoons fresh herbs

1 tablespoon fresh chives, chopped

1 tablespoon fresh parsley, chopped

1 loaf ciabatta (whole wheat if possible)

1. Preheat oven to 400°F.
2. Cut a 20" piece of parchment.
3. Line a baking sheet with aluminum foil.
4. Place butter and garlic in a glass bowl and cook in the microwave for about 2 minutes.
5. Mix all herbs into butter.
6. Slice the ciabatta into ½"-thick slices.
7. Spoon small amounts of herb butter onto both sides of each slice, smearing it around with a spoon.
8. Reshape the loaf on the parchment.
9. Fold the parchment.
10. Bake for 25 minutes. Slice and serve.

Calories: 153 | Fat: 8 g | Protein: 3 g | Sodium: 270 mg | Carbohydrates: 17 g | Fiber: 1 g

Baby Red Potatoes with Rosemary and Garlic

Serves 4

Rosemary and garlic provide a nice counterpoint to the sweetness of baby red potatoes in this recipe. A little Parmesan cheese certainly doesn't hurt either!

20 baby red potatoes, thinly sliced

2 cloves garlic, chopped

4 tablespoons butter, cut into small pieces

Salt and pepper to taste

½ teaspoon rosemary

¼ cup Parmesan cheese

1. Preheat oven to 400°F.
2. Cut a 20" piece of parchment.
3. Line a baking sheet with aluminum foil.
4. Toss all ingredients together on a piece of parchment.
5. Fold the parchment.
6. Bake for 40 minutes, shaking the package about halfway through to kind of mix things up.
7. Open the package and bake for another 10 minutes, then serve.

Calories: 402 | Fat: 14 g | Protein: 10 g | Sodium: 236 mg | Carbohydrates: 61 g | Fiber: 7.5 g

Savannah Red Rice

Serves 4

I loved visiting the city of Savannah. And the red rice we had there was delicious. In this version I use chopped prosciutto instead of the traditional bacon, but if you have bacon on hand, by all means, use it.

2 cups cooked brown rice

½ of medium red bell pepper, diced

¼ teaspoon onion powder

Salt and pepper to taste

1 cup canned diced tomatoes

2 slices prosciutto, diced

2 tablespoons ketchup

1 cup tomato sauce

1. Preheat oven to 400°F.
2. Cut a 20" piece of parchment.
3. Line a baking sheet with aluminum foil.
4. Place all ingredients in a bowl and mix.
5. Place mixture on parchment paper.
6. Fold the parchment.
7. Bake for 20 minutes.
8. Allow packet to rest several minutes before opening.
9. Sprinkle with Parmesan cheese if desired.

Calories: 342 | Fat: 4.5 g | Protein: 5 g | Sodium: 680 mg | Carbohydrates: 28 g | Fiber: 4 g

Israeli Couscous with Peas and Mint

Serves 4

Israeli couscous, or pearl couscous, is more like Italian orzo than traditional couscous. It has a texture that closely resembles that of pasta. Combine with peas and mint, and you've got the quintessential spring side dish.

5 ounces Israeli couscous, cooked in the microwave according to package instructions

1 cup frozen peas

20 fresh mint leaves, thinly sliced

1 tablespoon olive oil

1 tablespoon minced onion

Salt and pepper to taste

1. Preheat oven to 400°F.
2. Cut a 20" piece of parchment.
3. Line a baking sheet with aluminum foil.
4. Place all ingredients on the parchment and gently mix together.
5. Fold the parchment.
6. Bake for 15 minutes.

Calories: 97 | Fat: 3.5 g | Protein: 3 g | Sodium: 42 mg | Carbohydrates: 15 g | Fiber: 2 g

Orange Teriyaki Shrimp with Rice Noodles

Serves 4

Another no-boil pasta dish that will amaze you! I just love the vibrant colors of this dish—orange, pink, and green. I like to serve this with a bowl of takeout wonton soup.

6 ounces rice noodles

1 pound medium shrimp, peeled and deveined

1 scallion, thinly sliced

1 medium clove garlic, chopped

¼ of a broccoli head, cut into tiny florets

1 single-serving container (4 ounces) mandarin oranges

⅓ cup teriyaki sauce

¼ cup soy sauce

1. Preheat oven to 400ºF.

2. Cut a 20" piece of parchment.

3. Line a baking sheet with aluminum foil.

4. Place the rice noodles in a large bowl.

5. Cover with cold water and allow them to soak for 15 minutes.

6. Remove the noodles and place them in the center of a piece of parchment.

7. Make a nest in the middle and place the shrimp in it.

8. Top with scallions, garlic, and broccoli.

9. Pour the mandarin oranges on top, juice and all.

10. Then drizzle on the teriyaki and soy sauces, being sure you get them on the shrimp and as much of the noodles as possible.

11. Fold the parchment.

12. Bake for 30 minutes.

Calories: 197 | Fat: 2 g | Protein: 22 g | Sodium: 1673 mg | Carbohydrates: 22 g | Fiber: 2.5 g

No-Mess Gnocchi

Serves 4

I love gnocchi but I don't like the sticky mess I end up with in the pot afterward. The gnocchi in this dish turns out absolutely perfectly—soft and tender with some crunch around the edges. Serve with additional cheese for the cheese-aholics at your table.

16 ounces frozen gnocchi

3 tablespoons olive oil

2 scallions, thinly sliced

¾ cup Parmesan cheese

Salt and pepper to taste

⅛ teaspoon dried ground sage

1. Preheat oven to 400°F.
2. Cut a 20" piece of parchment.
3. Line a baking sheet with aluminum foil.
4. Place half of the gnocchi on the parchment.
5. Top with half the oil, half the scallions, and half the cheese.
6. Season with salt and pepper.
7. Place the rest of the gnocchi on top of the first layer and cover with remaining oil, scallions, cheese, and the sage.
8. Salt and pepper again.
9. Fold the parchment.
10. Bake for 30 minutes.

Calories: 320 | Fat: 17 g | Protein: 13 g | Sodium: 294 mg | Carbohydrates: 29 g | Fiber: 0 g

Chanukah Bread

Serves 8–10

Many years ago I saw Hal Linden (of Barney Miller fame) make a dish like this on a daytime talk show. Over the years the recipe has become my own and is something my family enjoys every holiday season. (Hal called it Chanukah Bread and even though my family isn't Jewish, that name has stuck!)

1 stick butter, softened

2 tablespoons olive oil

⅔ cup minced onion

6 tablespoons country-style Dijon mustard

2 tablespoons poppy seeds

4 tablespoons lemon juice

1 loaf sliced Italian bread (you could use plain white or wheat bread)

About 7–10 slices reduced-fat Swiss and American cheese (you want ½ slice of each per each slice of bread in your loaf)

1. Preheat oven to 375°F.

2. Cut a 30" piece of parchment.

3. Line a baking sheet with aluminum foil.

4. Mix the butter, oil, onion, mustard, poppy seeds, and lemon juice together.

5. Place the bread on the parchment.

6. Using a knife or small spatula, spread the butter mixture on one side of every slice of bread, reserving enough to spread all across the top of the bread.

7. Place half a slice each of Swiss and American between each slice of bread.

8. Smear the remaining butter mixture across the top.

9. Fold the parchment.

10. Bake for at least 30 minutes or until all the cheese is melted (it could take up to 15 minutes more if the cheese slices are thick or the loaf is very large).

Calories: 225 | Fat: 14 g | Protein: 6 g | Sodium: 300 mg | Carbohydrates: 15 g | Fiber: 1 g

Pastina with Spinach and Feta

Serves 4

The smallest type of pasta that's produced, pastina looks just like couscous. When combined with spinach and feta cheese, it makes for a delicious side dish or vegetarian entrée.

½ cup pastina

2 cups water

2 cloves garlic, chopped

1 cup fresh baby spinach leaves

½ cup feta cheese

½ teaspoon fresh oregano or ¼ teaspoon dried Italian herbs

Salt and pepper to taste

1 tablespoon olive oil

1. Preheat oven to 400°F.
2. Cut a 20" piece of parchment.
3. Line a baking sheet with aluminum foil.
4. Spray the center of the parchment.
5. Place pastina and water in a glass bowl and microwave on high for 7 minutes.
6. Remove and fluff with a fork.
7. Stir in all the other ingredients and place on the parchment.
8. Fold the parchment.
9. Bake for 17 minutes.
10. Fluff with a fork before serving.

Calories: 97 | Fat: 6 g | Protein: 5 g | Sodium: 265 mg | Carbohydrates: 6.5 g | Fiber: 0.5 g

Ravioli with Italian Sausage

Serves 2

Malleable dishes give you so much leeway to flex your creative muscles in the kitchen. With this recipe, feel free to use meatballs instead of the Italian sausage. Sometimes I add some frozen chopped spinach that has been defrosted and squeezed dry. And if fresh basil is hard to come by, dried basil will do the trick.

1 9-ounce package refrigerated fresh ravioli (any variety you like)

1 Italian sausage link, chopped

1½ cups prepared tomato sauce

1 tablespoon chopped fresh basil

1 tablespoon water

¼ cup fresh mozzarella

1. Preheat oven to 400°F.

2. Cut a 20" piece of parchment.

3. Line a baking sheet with aluminum foil.

4. Place the ravioli on the parchment.

5. Top with the sausage.

6. Pour the sauce on top.

7. Sprinkle the basil over the mixture and drizzle the water on top.

8. Fold the parchment.

9. Bake for 20 minutes.

10. Open the packet and break off and drop teaspoon-sized pieces of the mozzarella over the top.

11. Leave the packet open and return to the oven for 5 minutes until the cheese melts.

Calories: 535 | Fat: 18 g | Protein: 24 g | Sodium: 597 mg | Carbohydrates: 71 g | Fiber: 4.5 g

Hot Green Bean and Red Potato Salad with Goat Cheese

Serves 4

Enjoy this recipe as a fun and exciting alternative to regular potato salad. The creaminess of the goat cheese makes it delightful. This dish is not good cold, though, so be sure to reheat any leftovers before you serve them.

1½ pounds red baby potatoes, cut into quarters

½ pound green beans, trimmed and cut into 1" pieces

1 tablespoon fresh chives, chopped

1 shallot, chopped

1 tablespoon fresh parsley, chopped

Salt and pepper to taste

5 tablespoons olive oil

3 teaspoons Dijon mustard

2 tablespoons white vinegar

4 ounces goat cheese

1. Preheat oven to 400°F.

2. Cut a 30" piece of parchment.

3. Line a baking sheet with aluminum foil.

4. Place the potatoes and beans on parchment.

5. Sprinkle with the chives, shallot, parsley, salt, and pepper.

6. In a small bowl mix the olive oil, Dijon mustard, and vinegar.

7. Drizzle mixture over the bean and potato mixture.

8. Crumble the goat cheese over the entire thing.

9. Use your hands or a spoon to toss the ingredients together well.

10. Fold the parchment.

11. Bake for 1 hour.

12. Allow the package to rest about 5 minutes.

13. Open the package and stir with a spoon, until the goat cheese is completely melted and distributed.

Calories: 401 | Fat: 25 g | Protein: 10 g | Sodium: 162 mg | Carbohydrates: 34 g | Fiber: 4.5 g

Pizza Rice

Serves 2

In the mood for pizza but lacking something to use for a crust? This accessible recipe uses rice instead of a dough crust and is a big hit with kids. It's also a sneaky way to get kids who think they only like white rice to eat some brown rice. But this isn't just for kids—adults love this recipe too.

2 cups cooked brown rice

1 cup pizza or spaghetti sauce

⅔ cup shredded part-skim mozzarella cheese

2 tablespoons Parmesan cheese

Toppings of your choice (pepperoni, mushrooms, sausage, spinach, anchovies, etc.)

1. Preheat oven to 400°F.
2. Cut a 20" piece of parchment.
3. Line a baking sheet with aluminum foil.
4. Place the rice on parchment and press it down to distribute it evenly over a 5" × 5" area.
5. Spread the sauce on top of the rice and sprinkle mozzarella and Parmesan on top of that.
6. Add toppings.
7. Fold the parchment.
8. Bake for 20 minutes.
9. Open the packet and bake for 5–7 minutes more until cheese begins to change color.

To switch things up and go Mexican, you can always substitute salsa for the spaghetti sauce, and Monterey jack, Cheddar, or *queso fresco* for the mozzarella. Chicken would make a great topper in that instance.

Calories: 634 | Fat: 18 g | Protein: 19 g | Sodium: 371 mg | Carbohydrates: 45 g | Fiber: 6 g

Baby Potatoes with Capers

Serves 4

Capers and red baby potatoes pair to perfection in this side dish, while the sour cream curdles as it cooks and creates a cheese-like appearance. Partially cooking the potatoes first in the microwave reduces time in the oven.

1 pound red baby potatoes

Salt and pepper to taste

2½ tablespoons butter, cut into pieces

⅛ cup drained capers

¼ cup light sour cream

1. Preheat oven to 400°F.
2. Cut a 30" piece of parchment.
3. Line a baking sheet with aluminum foil.
4. Prick the potatoes and cook in the microwave on High for 3 minutes.
5. Cut the potatoes in half and place on the parchment.
6. Season with salt and pepper. Add butter, capers, and sour cream, tossing to combine.
7. Fold the parchment.
8. Bake for 30 minutes.

Calories: 173 | Fat: 9 g | Protein: 3.5 g | Sodium: 219 mg | Carbohydrates: 19 g | Fiber: 2.5 g

Naan Pizza with Leftovers

Serves 1

Think of this as more of a guideline than a hard-and-fast recipe. Using a piece of whole wheat naan bread, you can create a delicious white pizza using many different chicken and vegetable leftovers from this book.

1 piece whole wheat naan bread

1 teaspoon olive oil and 1 small clove garlic, chopped, OR 1 tablespoon prepared pesto sauce (decide which to use based on the chicken leftovers you select, thinking about which flavors would taste best together)

⅔ cup cheese (your choice of part-skim mozzarella, Cheddar, Monterey jack, goat cheese, fontina)

¼–¾ cup leftover vegetables (cooked spinach or chard works perfectly; cooked portobello mushroom is another excellent option)

½–¾ cup sliced leftover chicken

1. Preheat oven to 400°F.

2. Cut a 20" piece of parchment.

3. Line a baking sheet with foil and parchment.

4. Place the naan on the parchment.

5. Spread the naan with either the olive oil and garlic mixture or the prepared pesto sauce.

6. Sprinkle the cheese on top.

7. Add the vegetables.

8. Top with the sliced chicken. Bake uncovered for about 15 minutes, until the cheese melts.

A traditional unleavened Indian flat bread (it does not contain yeast), naan is now readily available at grocery stores.

Sesame Soba Noodles

Serves 2

Soba noodles are made with buckwheat and have a nice nutty texture. The flavors of peanut butter and sesame complement the noodles exceptionally well. The cucumber garnish gives the dish a fresh finish.

6 ounces soba noodles

2 cloves garlic, chopped

¼ cup creamy peanut butter

¼ cup tamari or soy sauce

¼ cup rice wine vinegar

2 teaspoons sesame oil

1 cup chicken broth

1 teaspoon toasted sesame seeds

1 baby cucumber, peeled and thinly sliced

1. Preheat the oven to 400°F.

2. Cut a 20" piece of parchment.

3. Line a baking sheet with aluminum foil.

4. Soak the noodles in very hot water in a big bowl for about 10 minutes.

5. In a glass bowl, combine garlic, peanut butter, soy, vinegar, oil, and broth. Microwave on High for about 2 minutes, until the peanut butter melts and you can get all the ingredients to mix.

6. Pour the mixture over the noodles and toss.

7. Fold the parchment.

8. Bake for 20 minutes.

9. Open the parchment and top with sesame seeds and cucumber slices. Toss to combine before serving.

Calories: 353 | Fat: 21 g | Protein: 19 g | Sodium: 2260 mg | Carbohydrates: 27 g | Fiber: 2.5 g

Biscuits with Pimiento Cheese

Serves 8

Get a double dose of Southern deliciousness with these two favorites combined into one. Some of the cheese may run out onto the parchment. Just use the biscuit to scoop it up and enjoy!

1 can jumbo canned biscuits (about 6 biscuits)

6 tablespoons pimiento cheese that has been refrigerated (see Beef and Pimiento Cheese Quesadillas in Chapter 4)

1. Preheat oven to 350°F.

2. Cut a 20" piece of parchment.

3. Line a baking sheet with foil and parchment.

4. Cut a slit along the side of each biscuit, very deep and almost through to the other side.

5. Place 1 tablespoon pimiento cheese in the middle in a ball and seal up the biscuit edges around it.

6. Place on parchment and leave parchment open.

7. Bake for 12 minutes or until golden brown and cooked through.

Calories: 219 | Fat: 11 g | Protein: 5.6 g | Sodium: 699 mg | Carbohydrates: 25 g | Fiber: 0 g

Rice Pilaf

Serves 4

In this recipe, just a few ingredients dress up rice so it suddenly becomes colorful and full of tasty tidbits. I prefer to use golden raisins, but you can substitute brown raisins if you prefer. This makes for a flavorful accompaniment to grilled fish or chicken.

¼ of a large onion, chopped

1 celery stalk, chopped

½ tablespoon olive oil, plus 1 tablespoon (reserved)

2 cups cooked brown rice

¼ cup golden raisins

¼ cup parsley, chopped

¼ cup slivered almonds

Salt and pepper to taste

1. Preheat oven to 400°F.

2. Cut a 20" piece of parchment.

3. Line a baking sheet with aluminum foil.

4. Place onion, celery, and ½ tablespoon olive oil in a glass measuring cup or glass bowl. Microwave on High for 2 minutes.

5. Place rice in the center of the parchment.

6. Top rice with vegetable mixture, 1 tablespoon oil, raisins, parsley, almonds, salt, and pepper. Gently mix all ingredients together with a spoon.

7. Fold the parchment.

8. Bake for 15 minutes.

Calories: 368 | Fat: 8 g | Protein: 4 g | Sodium: 25 mg | Carbohydrates: 27 g | Fiber: 3 g

"Scalloped" Ham and Potatoes

Serves 2

Ham and potatoes go so well together, particularly when they are scalloped (essentially, baked with butter and cream). Enjoy the flavors of scalloped ham and potatoes without a messy pan to scrub!

2 large baking potatoes, peeled and sliced into ¼" slices

¼ cup chopped ham

A generous ¼ cup shredded Cheddar cheese

½ teaspoon chives

¼ teaspoon onion powder

Salt and pepper to taste

3 tablespoons melted butter

⅛ cup cream

¼ cup skim milk

1 tablespoon Parmesan cheese

1. Preheat oven to 400°F.
2. Cut a 20" piece of parchment.
3. Line a baking sheet with aluminum foil.
4. Spray the parchment with cooking spray.
5. Place half of the potatoes in a 5"× 5" square.
6. Sprinkle on half of the ham, half the Cheddar, half the chives, and half the onion powder. Season with salt and pepper.
7. Drizzle on half the butter, half the cream, and half the milk.
8. Place other half of the potatoes on top, and repeat the steps above.
9. Top with the Parmesan cheese.
10. Fold the parchment.
11. Bake for 20 minutes.
12. Open the packet and broil for 3 minutes.

Calories: 574 | Fat: 34 g | Protein: 15 g | Sodium: 626 mg | Carbohydrates: 54 g | Fiber: 5 g

Couscous with Zucchini Ribbons

Serves 2 or 3

Zucchini ribbons give you a fun way to serve this old standby vegetable. The colorful ribbons mixed with the couscous makes a festive dish sure to interest everyone at your table.

1 cup water

1 cup couscous

1 tablespoon olive oil

Salt and pepper to taste

1 teaspoon Italian seasoning

⅛ teaspoon garlic powder

1 small zucchini

1. Preheat oven to 400°F.
2. Cut a 20" piece of parchment.
3. Line a baking sheet with aluminum foil.
4. Boil the water in a glass bowl in the microwave.
5. Add couscous and stir, then cover with plastic wrap and allow to stand 1–2 minutes.
6. Remove plastic wrap and stir the couscous.
7. Place the couscous on the parchment, add olive oil, and season with salt, pepper, herbs, and garlic powder.
8. Using a vegetable peeler, peel off long slices from the zucchini, peeling down until you reach the seeds.
9. Add zucchini to the couscous and toss mixture.
10. Fold the parchment.
11. Bake for 20 minutes.

Calories: 99 | Fat: 4.5 g | Protein: 2 g | Sodium: 3 mg | Carbohydrates: 15 g | Fiber: 1 g

CHAPTER 8

Desserts

Desserts are easy to make in parchment paper packets or on top of a sheet of parchment. In fact, you can use parchment to make all of your baking easier (use it when you make cookies so you don't have to wash the baking sheet). In this section, you'll find easy, fast, and yummy desserts using parchment—none of which require heavy-duty baking or mixing bowls. These recipes are meant to be quick and appealing and made fairly quickly in an oven or toaster oven.

Chocolate Chip Strawberry Pizza

Serves 6–8

Want to know my idea of the perfect marriage? Chocolate and strawberries. There's nothing like the taste of homemade chocolate chip cookies, but premade dough also works to create a yummy base for this easy dessert pizza.

16 ounces (or 1½ cups) chocolate chip cookie dough (store-bought or homemade)

4 ounces mascarpone cheese

¼ cup powdered sugar

1½ cups strawberries, washed, hulled, and thinly sliced

¼ cup strawberry jelly or jam

Powdered sugar (for garnish)

1. Preheat oven to 400°F.

2. Line a baking sheet with foil and parchment.

3. Place all of the cookie dough on the parchment.

4. Using your hands or a rolling pin, press out the dough to a rough 10" circle. It doesn't need to be perfect!

5. Using your fingers, pinch the edges to create a raised edge like a pizza crust.

6. Bake uncovered for 20 minutes.

7. While this is baking, mix the mascarpone cheese and powdered sugar in a small bowl. Remove the dough from oven and immediately spread the cheese and sugar mixture over it using a knife or offset spatula.

8. Arrange the sliced strawberries over the pizza.

9. Place strawberry jam or jelly in a small glass bowl and microwave for about 30 seconds, or until it becomes soft and easy to spread.

10. Using a pastry brush, brush the jelly or jam over the berries.

11. Allow the pizza to rest for at least 30 minutes.

12. Dust the top with powdered sugar.

13. Slice and serve.

Calories: 344 | Fat: 16 g | Protein: 4.5 g | Sodium: 144 mg | Carbohydrates: 51 g | Fiber: 1.5 g

Stuffed Bananas

Serves 4

This dessert tastes like a warm, wonderful pudding. It's quick to prep and tastes far more complex than you'd think it would! Use whatever kind of chocolate floats your boat.

4 ripe bananas

4 pieces good-quality chocolate (about ⅓ of an ounce apiece)

2 teaspoons cinnamon sugar

4 teaspoons prepared caramel sauce

½ cup whipped cream

1. Preheat the oven to 400°F.
2. Cut a 30" piece of parchment.
3. Line a baking sheet with aluminum foil.
4. Peel the bananas and lay them on the parchment.
5. Break each piece of chocolate (one per banana) into about 6–8 pieces.
6. Push the chocolate pieces into the bananas at even intervals.
7. Sprinkle the bananas with cinnamon sugar.
8. Drizzle 1 teaspoon of caramel sauce over each banana.
9. Fold the parchment.
10. Bake for about 7 minutes or until the chocolate is melted.
11. Serve with whipped cream.

I keep a shaker of cinnamon sugar mix in my cupboard. My kids use it to shake on buttered toast, and I grab it for desserts like this one. To make one, mix ¼ cup granulated sugar with 2 teaspoons cinnamon and store in a clean spice shaker.

Calories: 257 | Fat: 5 g | Protein: 3.5 g | Sodium: 16 mg | Carbohydrates: 58 g | Fiber: 6 g

Baked Apple

Serves 1

These instructions are for one serving, but make as many as you need. These baked apples are fragrant and filling fresh out of the oven and taste just as good cold the next day.

1 apple, cored

2 tablespoons brown sugar

1 teaspoon cinnamon

Pinch of salt

½ tablespoon melted butter

2 tablespoons chopped pecans

2 tablespoons water, apple juice, or apple cider

1. Preheat oven to 400°F.
2. Cut a 12" piece of parchment.
3. Line a baking sheet with aluminum foil.
4. Place the apple on the parchment.
5. Mix remaining ingredients then stuff them down inside the center of the apple.
6. Allow excess ingredients to mound around the bottom of the apple.
7. Fold the parchment and bake for an hour and a half.
8. Be sure to spoon out all the gooey sauce that has formed on the bottom of the parchment!

Calories: 313 | Fat: 16 g | Protein: 1.5 g | Sodium: 70 mg | Carbohydrates: 46 g | Fiber: 4 g

Baked Cinnamon-Sugar Pineapple with Pudding

Serves 1

At a friend's house once I sampled an Indian family specialty—rice pudding with fruit and spices. I never got the recipe, but I re-created the flavors in this dish.

1 pineapple ring

Cinnamon sugar

Maraschino cherry and juice

½ cup store-bought rice pudding

1. Preheat oven to 400°F.
2. Line a baking sheet with foil and parchment.
3. Cover a baking sheet with parchment paper.
4. Place the pineapple ring on the parchment.
5. Cover the top with cinnamon sugar.
6. Place a maraschino cherry in the center.
7. Drizzle 2 teaspoons maraschino cherry juice over the pineapple.
8. Bake for 15 minutes, with parchment unfolded.
9. Serve warm, on top of the rice pudding.

Calories: 101 | Fat: 1 g | Protein: 2 g | Sodium: 62 mg | Carbohydrates: 22 g | Fiber: 0.5 g

Baked Banana Split

Serves 1

Banana splits aren't just for ice cream! This baked banana dish offers all of the flavors of a banana split with fewer calories. Of course, if you want to, you can serve this over ice cream— it's sinfully delicious either way.

1 banana, split lengthwise

1 tablespoon Nutella

1 tablespoon strawberry jam

½ cup pineapple chunks

½ individual-size vanilla pudding cup

1. Preheat oven to 400°F.
2. Cut a 12" piece of parchment.
3. Line a baking sheet with aluminum foil.
4. Place the banana on the parchment paper.
5. Spread the Nutella on the banana.
6. Spread the jam over the Nutella.
7. Place the pineapple on top.
8. Fold the parchment.
9. Bake for 10 minutes.
10. Open the packet and dollop the pudding on top (you could also use ice cream if you prefer). To dress it up, you can drizzle the top with chocolate or add a maraschino cherry.

You're likely already familiar with Nutella, a heavenly chocolate hazelnut spread that originated in Italy. If not, look for it next to the peanut butter in your market.

Calories: 458 | Fat: 10 g | Protein: 6 g | Sodium: 423 mg | Carbohydrates: 89 g | Fiber: 6 g

Peachy Sugar Cookies

Serves 8–12

This quick dessert mimics peach pie. Although the recipe uses prepared sugar cookie dough, you could use homemade. The next time you make sugar cookies, just freeze some of the dough and keep it on hand for this simple dessert.

16 ounces prepared refrigerated sugar cookie dough

2 15-ounce cans halved peaches in light syrup

Cinnamon to taste

1. Preheat oven to 350ºF.
2. Line a baking sheet with foil and parchment.
3. Break the sugar cookie dough into small pieces.
4. Flatten two pieces together to about the size of a peach half.
5. Place the flattened dough on the parchment.
6. Top with a peach half (flat-side down).
7. Sprinkle peach and cookie dough with cinnamon (at least ¼ teaspoon).
8. Flatten another cookie piece and drape it over the top of the peach.
9. Repeat using all the dough and peaches.
10. Bake unfolded for 17 minutes.

Calories: 127 | Fat: 5 g | Protein: 1 g | Sodium: 107 mg | Carbohydrates: 19 g | Fiber: 1 g

Rustic Apple Tart

Serves 4–6

This easy version of apple pie delivers a colorful dessert that smells incredible as it bakes. Be sure to slice the apples very thinly so they can cook completely. This is to die for with a small scoop of vanilla ice cream or frozen yogurt.

1 refrigerated unbaked pie crust

1 tablespoon butter

2 tablespoons apple butter

2 apples, cored and sliced thin

2 teaspoons cinnamon

3 tablespoons sugar

Pinch salt

1. Preheat oven to 400°F.
2. Line a baking sheet with foil and parchment.
3. Place the pie crust on the parchment and scrunch the edges to create a crust, turning the crust into a square.
4. Melt butter in a small glass bowl in the microwave.
5. Stir in the apple butter.
6. Spread this mixture over the pie crust. Arrange apples on top in neat rows.
7. In a small bowl mix cinnamon, sugar, and salt.
8. Sprinkle on top of the apples.
9. Place a piece of parchment on top of the tart.
10. Bake unfolded for 35 minutes.

Apple butter is very concentrated applesauce. It has a lovely brown color due to the caramelization of the apples. You can find it in the jam and jelly section of your grocery store.

Calories: 163 | Fat: 9 g | Protein: 1 g | Sodium: 156 mg | Carbohydrates: 20 g | Fiber: 1 g

Poppy Seed Baklava

Serves 4

Little effort delivers delicious decadence with this dessert. Canned poppy seed filling can be found in the baking aisle, but it's also available online if you don't have luck finding it at your local store. The filo may crumble a bit when you cut it, but this tastes so good, no one will mind.

6 sheets filo dough

5 tablespoons butter

¼ cup canned poppy seed filling

½ cup ground walnuts

1 teaspoon cinnamon

Cinnamon sugar

1. Preheat oven to 350°F.
2. Line a baking sheet with foil and parchment.
3. Place 3 sheets of filo in a stack on the parchment.
4. Melt the butter in a glass bowl in the microwave. Stir the poppy seed filling, nuts, and cinnamon into the butter.
5. Spread ⅓ of the filling mixture over half of the top sheet of filo.
6. Fold the unused half of the filo stack over the coated half.
7. Spread another ⅓ of the filling mixture on the filo.
8. Top with 3 more sheets and spread the last ⅓ of the filling on half of the top sheet.
9. Fold the unused half over the filling.
10. Spray the top sheet with cooking spray. Sprinkle cinnamon sugar on top.
11. Bake unfolded for 20 minutes.
12. Cut into squares and serve.

Traditional baklava is a Turkish dish made up of layers of filo dough interspersed with honey and nuts. This dish has much less sugar than the classic, which is loaded with honey.

Calories: 513 | Fat: 45 g | Protein: 7 g | Sodium: 257 mg | Carbohydrates: 24 g | Fiber: 3 g

S'mores Crepes

Serves 1

This recipe is an all-time favorite in my house—particularly in the winter, when s'mores made over a campfire feel like eons away. You can find prepared crepes in your grocery store; that's the key to super-simple and quick assembly for this dessert.

1 crepe

½ of a 1.55-ounce milk chocolate candy bar, broken into ½" pieces

¼ cup mini marshmallows

¼ of a graham cracker quadrant, crumbled

Powdered sugar

1. Preheat oven to 400°F.
2. Cut a 12" piece of parchment.
3. Line a baking sheet with aluminum foil.
4. Place the crepe on the parchment.
5. Line up the chocolate on one end of the crepe.
6. Add the marshmallows and crumbled graham cracker on top and around the chocolate.
7. Roll up the crepe, starting at the edge with the chocolate. Place seam-side down on the parchment.
8. Fold the parchment.
9. Bake for 5 minutes.
10. Dust with powdered sugar before serving.

Calories: 413 | Fat: 13 g | Protein: 6 g | Sodium: 404 mg | Carbohydrates: 69 g | Fiber: 2.5 g

Peanut Butter S'mores Crepes

Serves 1

Here's a nutty take on the original S'mores Crepe recipe—I just couldn't resist adding a variation! I like to use crunchy peanut butter for that added bit of a texture, but creamy tastes just sinful.

1 crepe

1 tablespoon organic peanut butter

½ of a 1.55-ounce milk chocolate candy bar, broken into ½" pieces

¼ cup mini marshmallows

¼ of a graham cracker quadrant, crumbled

Powdered sugar

1. Preheat oven to 400°F.

2. Cut a 12" piece of parchment.

3. Line a baking sheet with aluminum foil.

4. Place the crepe on the parchment.

5. Spread the peanut butter on the crepe (covering as much as possible, but not the whole thing).

6. Line up the chocolate on one end of the crepe.

7. Add the marshmallows and crumbled graham cracker on top and around the chocolate.

8. Roll up the crepe, starting at the edge with the chocolate. Place seam-side down on the parchment.

9. Fold the parchment.

10. Bake for 5 minutes.

11. Dust with powdered sugar before serving.

Calories: 513 | Fat: 22 g | Protein: 10 g | Sodium: 461 mg | Carbohydrates: 70 g | Fiber: 3 g

Mini Fruit Pies

Serves 1

Who knew fruit pies could be so tasty? And so very cute! This recipe uses little sponge cake dessert cups to create the perfect serving size.

1 sponge cake dessert cup

Scant ¼ cup canned fruit pie filling

1 tablespoon crumb topping

1. Preheat the oven to 400°F.
2. Cover a baking sheet with parchment paper.
3. Scoop out the inside of the dessert cup (discarding it), leaving at least ½" thickness around the edges and bottom.
4. Place the cup on the parchment and fill with fruit pie filling.
5. Top with crumb topping.
6. Bake uncovered for 10–12 minutes, until lightly browned on the top.

I make up big batches of crumb topping in my food processor and keep it in the freezer to use for muffin and pie toppings. You can easily make a small batch in a bowl by mixing ¼ stick softened butter, ¼ cup sugar, and ¼ cup flour.

Calories: 329 | Fat: 5 g | Protein: 5 g | Sodium: 216 mg | Carbohydrates: 66 g | Fiber: 1 g

Strawberry Dark Chocolate Crepes

Serves 1

If you like strawberries dipped in chocolate, you'll love this simple and fabulous dessert. It's also good with blueberry jam and fresh blueberries.

1 crepe

1 tablespoon strawberry jam

½ ounce dark chocolate, broken into pieces

2 fresh strawberries, hulled, sliced, and several additional whole berries

Whipped cream to taste

Chocolate sauce to taste

1. Preheat oven to 400°F.
2. Cut a 12" piece of parchment.
3. Line a baking sheet with aluminum foil.
4. Place the crepe on the parchment.
5. Spread the jam around as much as possible.
6. Line up the chocolate pieces on one edge of the crepe.
7. Top with the strawberries.
8. Roll up the crepe, starting at the edge with the chocolate. Place seam-side down on the parchment.
9. Fold the parchment.
10. Bake for 7 minutes.
11. Serve with whipped cream, chocolate sauce, and additional berries.

Calories: 215 | Fat: 6 g | Protein: 3 g | Sodium: 246 mg | Carbohydrates: 39 g | Fiber: 2.5 g

Puff Pastry Shells with Chocolate, Vanilla Pudding, and Strawberries

Serves 1

Puff pastry shells define decadence and require skill to make from scratch—so don't give away your secret (they're store-bought; look for them in the frozen dessert section of your grocery store). You can vary this recipe by using dark chocolate and substituting raspberries or blueberries for the strawberries.

1 puff pastry shell (don't defrost, but it's fine for this to sit on the baking sheet while you assemble ingredients)

2 squares of a 1.55-ounce milk chocolate bar

2 strawberries, hulled and sliced

2 tablespoons vanilla pudding

Chocolate sauce for serving

Powdered sugar for serving

1. Preheat oven to 350ºF.

2. Cover a baking sheet with parchment paper.

3. Place the shell on the parchment paper.

4. Bake uncovered for 20 minutes.

5. Remove from oven and pull or cut off (if it doesn't want to come off) the "lid" of the shell.

6. Place chocolate inside of the shell and return to oven for 5 minutes, uncovered, or until shell is golden brown and the chocolate is melted.

7. Smooth the chocolate around the inside of the shell and spread a little on the inside of the lid.

8. Place half of the berries in the shell, and top with the pudding.

9. Top with the remaining berries and place the lid on top.

10. Drizzle with chocolate sauce and/or dust with powdered sugar to serve.

Calories: 277 | Fat: 16 g | Protein: 4 g | Sodium: 202 mg | Carbohydrates: 30 g | Fiber: 1.5 g

Clementine Tart

Serves 6–8

With this recipe, you cook macadamia nuts right into the crust, giving it a more complex flavor profile. And the pieces of clementine are so sweet and juicy they feel like a burst of sunshine!

1 refrigerated pie crust

⅓ cup chopped macadamia nuts

⅓ cup semisweet chocolate chips

3 individual-size vanilla pudding cups

3 clementines, peeled and broken into individual segments, with pith (white parts) removed

⅓ cup orange marmalade

Chocolate sauce for serving

1. Preheat oven to temperature directed by pie crust package.

2. Line a baking sheet with foil and parchment.

3. Place crust on the parchment. Scrunch up the edges of the crust to make a barrier, creating a square. Scatter the nuts on the crust and press them into it.

4. Loosely cover with a piece of parchment and bake for half the time directed on the pie crust package.

5. Remove the parchment, sprinkle the chocolate chips over the crust, and bake uncovered the rest of the time as directed.

6. Remove from the oven and spread the chocolate using a knife. Don't worry if the chocolate doesn't completely cover the crust or is a bit chunky.

7. Allow to cool. Top with the pudding. Arrange the clementines on top.

8. Microwave the marmalade in a glass bowl for about 20 seconds and then drizzle or brush on the clementines. Drizzle the chocolate sauce over the tart.

Calories: 334 | Fat: 15 g | Protein: 4 g | Sodium: 415 mg | Carbohydrates: 48 g | Fiber: 1.5 g

Chocolate Bread Pudding

Serves 3 or 4

Warm, moist, and slightly crunchy on top with a hint of cinnamon, this fragrant dessert will amaze you with how simply it comes together. I like to use whole wheat bread in this recipe, but that's up to your personal preference.

4 thick slices of a crusty bread, cut into squares

1 cup skim milk

1 egg

Pinch of salt

2 tablespoons butter

1.5 ounces bittersweet chocolate, chopped or in chip form

2 tablespoons sugar

Cinnamon sugar (optional)

1. Preheat oven to 400°F.
2. Cut a 20" piece of parchment.
3. Line a baking sheet with aluminum foil.
4. Place the bread in a medium bowl and add milk, egg, and salt and stir to mix.
5. Place the butter and chocolate in a small glass bowl and microwave on High for 30 seconds. Stir until all chocolate is dissolved.
6. Add the sugar to the chocolate mixture; stir.
7. Pour chocolate over the bread mixture; stir.
8. Allow bread mixture to soak for about 5 minutes.
9. Place mixture on the parchment.
10. Fold the parchment.
11. Bake for 15 minutes.
12. Open the packet and sprinkle with cinnamon sugar, if desired.
13. Leave the packet open and return to oven for another 10 minutes.

Calories: 275 | Fat: 15 g | Protein: 7 g | Sodium: 240 mg | Carbohydrates: 28 g | Fiber: 0.5 g

Dessert Cups with Rice Pudding and Blueberries

Serves 1

Dessert cups make another appearance, this time to hold pudding and fruit. You can play with this concept, using any kind of pudding and any kind of fruit. This dessert looks perfectly put together, as if you spent ages preparing it.

1 sponge cake dessert cup

Scant ¼ cup store-bought rice pudding

10 blueberries (fresh or frozen)

½ teaspoon cinnamon sugar

1. Preheat oven to 400°F.

2. Line a baking sheet with foil and parchment.

3. Scoop out the center of the dessert cup (discarding the center), leaving at least ½" on the bottom and sides.

4. Place the cup on the parchment and fill with pudding.

5. Top with blueberries and cinnamon sugar.

6. Bake unfolded for 10 minutes.

Calories: 238 | Fat: 4 g | Protein: 5 g | Sodium: 160 mg | Carbohydrates: 45 g | Fiber: 1 g

Caramel Pears

Serves 2

These caramel pears provide a warm, sweet ending to any meal. Serve them alone or as a topping for ice cream or frozen yogurt. Bosc pears work best for this recipe, but substitute other varieties if Bosc aren't available at your market.

1 Bosc pear, peeled, cored, and sliced

¼ cup prepared caramel sauce

1. Preheat oven to 400ºF.
2. Cut a 12" piece of parchment.
3. Line a baking sheet with aluminum foil.
4. Place the pear on the center of the parchment and top with caramel sauce.
5. Fold the parchment.
6. Bake for 35 minutes.

Calories: 103 | Fat: 2 g | Protein: 1.5 g | Sodium: 49 mg | Carbohydrates: 22 g | Fiber: 2.5 g

Peach Waffle Bowls

Serves 1

Who said waffle bowls could only carry ice cream? Here they make the ideal base for a peachy dessert. You could use canned pears in place of the canned peaches for a variation—or go crazy and mix the two! Experiment and have fun with this one.

1 waffle bowl

1 tablespoon prepared caramel sauce

1½ tablespoons crumb topping (see Mini Fruit Pies in this chapter for an easy recipe)

⅛ teaspoon cinnamon

1 individual-size vanilla pudding cup (room temperature)

5 slices canned peaches

1. Preheat the oven to 400°F.

2. Line a baking sheet with foil and parchment.

3. Place bowl on the parchment.

4. Pour the caramel sauce into the waffle bowl and swirl to coat the bottom.

5. Mix the crumb topping with the cinnamon and place about ½ tablespoon on top of the caramel.

6. Add the pudding to the bowl.

7. Top with peaches.

8. Sprinkle remaining crumb topping on the peaches.

9. Bake uncovered for 10 minutes.

Calories: 347 | Fat: 6 g | Protein: 8 g | Sodium: 421 mg | Carbohydrates: 70 g | Fiber: 3.5 g

Easy Indian Corn Pudding

Serves 2

A New England specialty, Indian corn pudding relies on a base of cornmeal. This version uses corn muffins to speed things up! The result is warming, perfect for a chilly autumn night.

4 mini store-bought corn muffins

1 teaspoon molasses

2 tablespoons nonfat plain yogurt

3 tablespoons vanilla pudding

1 tablespoon prepared caramel sauce

1. Preheat the oven to 400°F.

2. Cut a 12" piece of parchment.

3. Line a baking sheet with aluminum foil.

4. Quarter the muffins and place them in the center of the parchment.

5. Drizzle muffins with molasses.

6. Top with yogurt, pudding, and caramel sauce. Gently mix.

7. Fold the parchment.

8. Bake for 15 minutes.

Calories: 296 | Fat: 8 g | Protein: 6 g | Sodium: 622 mg | Carbohydrates: 47 g | Fiber: 2 g

Croissant Surprise

Serves 2

A warm, flaky croissant with melted Nutella and fresh raspberries makes an incredible dessert sandwich. If you can't find mini croissants, get one large croissant and cut it in half to serve two people.

2 mini croissants or 1 large (cut either size in half like a sandwich roll)

1 tablespoon Nutella

10 raspberries (fresh or frozen)

1. Preheat oven to 400°F.
2. Cut a 12" piece of parchment.
3. Line a baking sheet with aluminum foil.
4. Spread Nutella on the cut sides of the croissants.
5. For each croissant, arrange raspberries on the bottom half and top with the "lid."
6. Fold the parchment.
7. Bake for 12 minutes.

Calories: 181 | Fat: 9 g | Protein: 3 g | Sodium: 215 mg | Carbohydrates: 22 g | Fiber: 3.5 g

INDEX

About the Author

Brette Sember blogs about parchment paper cooking at *www.NoPotCooking.com*.
   She also writes the popular food blog *www.MarthaAndMe.net*. She is the author of an upcoming book called *Cookie* from University Press of Florida, a fun history of cookies and their impact on American life. Look for her other upcoming titles, including *The Organized Kitchen* and *The Muffin Tin Cookbook* from Adams Media. She lives in Buffalo, NY, with her husband, two children, and two golden retrievers. Her website is *www.BretteSember.com* and you can follow her on Twitter @BretteSember. Stop by her NoPotCooking.com blog for more recipe ideas, to share comments on your favorite recipes from the book, or offer your own parchment paper cooking recipes.

the hungry Editor

Foodies Unite!

Bring your appetite and follow The Hungry Editor who really loves to eat. She'll be discussing (and drooling over) all things low-fat and full-fat, local and fresh, canned and frozen, highbrow and lowbrow. . .

When it comes to good eats, The Hungry Editor (and her tastebuds) do not discriminate!

It's a Feeding Frenzy—dig in!

Sign up for our newsletter at

www.adamsmedia.com/blog/cooking

and download our free **Top Ten Gourmet Meals for $7** recipes!